The War Came to Me

A Story of Endurance and Survival

Eva Broessler Weissman
and
Gregory Moore

UNIVERSITY PRESS OF AMERICA,® INC.
Lanham • Boulder • New York • Toronto • Plymouth, UK

Copyright © 2009 by
University Press of America,® Inc.
4501 Forbes Boulevard
Suite 200
Lanham, Maryland 20706
UPA Acquisitions Department (301) 459-3366

Estover Road
Plymouth PL6 7PY
United Kingdom

All rights reserved
Printed in the United States of America
British Library Cataloging in Publication Information Available

Library of Congress Control Number: 2009931151
ISBN: 978-0-7618-4689-5 (paperback : alk. paper)

∞™ The paper used in this publication meets the minimum
requirements of American National Standard for Information
Sciences—Permanence of Paper for Printed Library Materials,
ANSI Z39.48—1984

This book is dedicated to the memory of Gustav and Thekla Broessler, the parents of Eva and Ruth, the Dutch families Simons and Isaac and to Eva's husband, Oscar Weissman.

Translation of inscription on wall relief located in the
Billrothgymnasium, Vienna, Austria

NOT TO HATE—
BUT TO LOVE
WE ARE HERE!

—SOPHOCLES

Contents

Foreword	vii
Prologue: A Book Is Born	ix
Acknowledgments	xiii
Introduction: A Kaleidoscope of Remembrances	xv
1 Growing Up in Austria	1
2 From Austria to The Netherlands	14
3 Trapped in The Netherlands	28
4 Ruth's Escape	43
5 Hidden in Plain Sight	54
6 Reunions	64
Epilogue: A Life with a View	77
Appendix	83
Selected Bibliography	93
Index	97
About the Authors	103

Foreword

There is in Eva a tenacity of spirit and pervasive charm that are immeasurably precious. How does one account for such characteristics? Are they arguably the result of experience, positive or negative? Could they be the shared inheritance of a humanist culture from the heart of Europe? Are they actually—although inimitable—a cause for hope that we collectively can share?

Among the many callings and professions, the most engaging are those which do not match some public mold or expectation, but instead exhibit the strong sense of original identification espoused by an individual, transformed into a charismatic driving-force.

Eva's story is more than an enumeration of remarkable and appalling circumstances, delays, oppositions, defeats, losses and discoveries that span much of the intense and desperate reality of these decades. It is the serious and engaging perhaps anguished smile, attempt and repeated attempt to forge a better future. The quick wit. The need to insist. The ability to reach the point of despair and then not to succumb.

Much of her explicit external world is that of intelligent interchange—the patient who charms her doctors before surgery and rewards them with a floral memento afterwards. The inventive succession of initiatives that make possible the furthering of relationships and causes. Her heart went out years ago toward a cause which is both a real one and represents an unreasonable challenge—how to combat inherited disease. She saw, without medical training, that there was a central opportunity.

I have often wondered why Eva's concern with Huntington's Disease has been just right for her. She has not inherited this genetic trait and in fact has been blessed by health, stamina, high intelligence, and qualities that are not readily summarized with a few adjectives. Is it because the challenge is unreasonable? Is there some parallel between the plight of the Huntington's patient and the displaced souls of the world whose lives have been uprooted by war: the colossus of man's abuse? Or is it the alarming realization that—even without a war—we must share our moments with others who have the conviction that the dimensions of our collective reality can change, that the goal is not only financial, not only to find a cure, but rather to participate in the surely endless process by which small enduring steps actually create?

It is a joy to be able to count myself among her friends.

Alan Tartakoff

Alan M. Tartakoff, Ph.D., is Professor of Pathology and Director of the Cell Biology Program at Case Western Reserve University in Cleveland, Ohio and, like Eva Weissman, a Past President/Life Director of the Huntington's Disease Society of America Northeast Ohio Chapter.

Prologue: A Book Is Born

It has been a long gestation period but, finally, the manuscript has gone to the publisher. Perfection should not be expected, but it is hoped that in its imperfection the book will somehow inform the readers of trials and tribulations as well as of sadness and joy experienced in daring and dreadful days. The book is intended to be a testament honoring the many whose efforts saved the lives of those who would otherwise have perished.

For many years, friends and relatives listened to my life's story and encouraged me to write an autobiography. Yet, daily activities became ever more important than starting the project. When almost ready to put remembrances on paper, a friend commented sarcastically on the recent rage of producing "ego documents." This remark I interpreted as indirect criticism and distasteful self-aggrandizement; it served as a further reason for me to delay writing an autobiography.

Rather than writing my autobiography, it was much easier and more enjoyable to have direct contact with children. I accepted invitations from local schools where teachers and students listened to my Holocaust stories, asked good questions, and even wrote touching notes of appreciation afterwards. This, after I had finally accepted being considered a "Holocaust survivor," even though I had fortunately not been in a concentration camp. I was lucky enough to have been reunited with my parents, Gustav and Thekla Broessler, and my sister, Ruth, after years of separation. I now know that my questioning the designation of "Holocaust survivor" was also based on a misinterpretation and on my own wrong criteria. Customarily, anybody who was persecuted by and survived the Nazi regime can rightfully be called "a Holocaust survivor."

In the summer of 2004, visiting my sister Ruth Newmark and her family in La Jolla, California, when I told family stories, they urged me to write down some special anecdotes. Reflecting on our November 1995 interviews for the Shoah Visual History Project, initiated by movie producer Steven Spielberg, Ruth and I felt that our interviews did not do justice to what we really wished to convey. We were not pleased with the result of the Shoah tapes as a legacy, perhaps due to our own reluctance to answer standard questions posed by the interviewer. How could our lives' experiences adequately be recorded in a few hours' interview? How can our harrowing experiences be meaningfully incorporated in a video or book? These are the questions that still plague me and why, above, I referred to this book's imperfections.

Just about the time I promised my family to start writing down some of our family anecdotes, Sister Mary Louise Trivison, S.N.D., invited me to Notre Dame College, in Cleveland, Ohio, as a guest speaker and to address a small class of her students. I began to feel confident to speak not only to high school but also to college students and even professors. Notre Dame College had first invited me as one of three speakers at its Holocaust Educators' Conference II in November 2001. I believe that being able to talk about my experiences to various audiences provided the impetus for an "ego document" without guilt and misinterpretation of the word.

Even better, through my contacts at Notre Dame College and its Tolerance Resource Center, I met Gregory Moore, Ph.D., Chair of the College's Department of History and Political Science. He envisioned that my story, combined with my sister's, had value for educational purposes.

This idea particularly appealed to me because the project offered an opportunity to write about a certain side of the Holocaust, showing the best and not the most evil of people. From the beginning Professor Moore and I planned to report how my parents, sister and I managed to escape the worst terrors of inhumanity with great good fortune and through the courageous efforts of others. In a modest way, this book should add to other Holocaust reports of eyewitnesses before my generation of survivors has dwindled away completely. In the main, the Holocaust as a historical event has received a great deal of world attention with much of the written works focused on the death camps as well as on other atrocities conducted by the Nazis and their sympathizers. By contrast, Professor Moore has attempted to show through a focus on my story that at least some Jews were spared the death camps through the help of persons willing to risk their own lives to save others from the horrors of Hitler's Final Solution.

With our commitment to the Moore/Weissman collaboration, a complete manuscript evolved. Dr. Alan Tartakoff was kind enough to provide the foreword. I wrote the prologue, introduction and epilogue, and Professor Moore wrote six chapters that form the nucleus of the book. The title *The War Came to Me: A Story of Endurance and Survival* is intended to refer particularly to

1938, the year Hitler annexed Austria, until May 1945, when World War II ended in The Netherlands, with the addition of the few postwar years leading to my sister's arrival in the United States in 1946 and my arrival in 1947. Both Professor Moore and I wanted to bring to light what led to these events through telling my and also my sister's story against its historic background. He did so as a historian and educator; my emphasis was on the remembrances of happenings that my immediate family, a family of four, endured and fortunately survived.

Having mentioned how this book was born, I would like to add that during the four years of Greg's and my collaboration new insights were gained and new relationships were formed. For me Professor Moore has become Greg as I, of course, am simply Eva. In 2005, we thought of having a complete manuscript. After careful review, however, we realized that much more could be done. Because of our busy lives, it took three more years to fully complete the manuscript, in 2008. Much verification and further research was accomplished, aided by my sister Ruth's scholarly approach and her superb editorial skills.

As co-authors Greg and I are delighted that University Press of America has offered to publish our manuscript.

Eva Broessler Weissman
July 2008
Lakewood, Ohio

Acknowledgments

Every book is a collaborative effort, and this one is no exception. Without the encouragement and help from numerous sources, this book would never have come about. Our thanks go first to the Jewish Community Federation in Cleveland, Ohio for providing a grant to assist with some of the expense of researching and writing this book. We are especially grateful to Eva's sister, Ruth Newmark, who generously provided us with her unpublished papers, additional research information, and her smart and candid editorial skills. These were invaluable in helping us tell Eva's story.

Thanks also to Mark Newmark, Eva's nephew, for his careful reading of the manuscript and editorial suggestions. Eva's niece, Katya Newmark, inspired the phrases "the war came to me" and "a life with a view." We wish to thank Janice Clayton at Eastern Kentucky University for her help in formatting the manuscript and indexing it. Thanks also to Dr. Kay Scarborough at EKU for putting us in touch with Janice. Judith Rothman and Brian DeRocco at University Press of America were most forthcoming in answering the questions we had about preparing the manuscript for publication.

The resources and students at Notre Dame College were most helpful in the preparation of this book. Students Stephanie Wagner and Andrew Boksansky assisted with research and have our gratitude for their help. Additional thanks go to Cindy Linn for her assistance with genealogical research. The Tolerance Resource Center on the campus of Notre Dame College provided many useful sources about the Holocaust and the German occupation of The Netherlands. And special thanks go to Sister Mary Louise Trivison, Professor Emerita of Theology and Spanish at Notre Dame College. Sister Trivison has worked tirelessly to bring people of diverse faiths together and has made awareness of the Holocaust and anti-Semitism a primary focus of the College's Tolerance Resource Center. It was her introduction of Beth Wesolowski Salem to Eva that led to the beginning of our effort to write this book.

Since then, Beth has been an integral part of all of this. Now a doctoral candidate at Case Western Reserve University, Beth introduced us to each other some three years ago and the result of that meeting led to this book. Additionally, Beth added her own keen editorial eye to the manuscript and put it in its final format for publication. None of this would have been possible without you, Beth. Thanks!

Introduction: A Kaleidoscope of Remembrances

A kaleidoscope contains various pieces reflected by mirrors with patterns that change when rotated. So perhaps this introduction is in many ways like a kaleidoscope. *The War Came To Me: A Story of Endurance and Survival* basically refers to the years 1938 until 1945. This is but a small fraction of my life but a very important one. Therefore, I am grateful that in the following chapters, Professor Moore has interwoven some of my and my sister's experiences into historic text so that the book can serve for educational purposes as well as for human interest for a general readership.

I am writing this introduction to provide autobiographical material that puts additional emphasis on the personal side of the story. I am elaborating mainly on the parts of my background that might have prepared me to cope with the adversities I encountered without physical or mental damage.

I entered the world in Vienna, Austria on September 27, 1923. This was the year when TIME, Inc. published the first issue of *Time Capsule*, an annual series of "A History of the year condensed from pages of TIME." This particular issue had a picture of the great actor Charlie Chaplin on the front cover and included chapters on American President Warren G. Harding's sudden death as well as Mussolini's first year in power in Italy and Hitler's abortive beer-hall putsch in Munich, Germany. The world was full of contradiction. Such contradiction was vividly expressed by Charlie Chaplin, whose performances in silent movies depicted tragedy as comedy. His role in *The Dictator*—especially as we know now—was nothing to laugh about as slapstick turned into reality.

1923 was only five years after the end of World War I, when Austria changed from being a collapsed monarchy to a democratic republic. Too young to feel the early aftereffects of World War I with rising inflation and accompanying hardships, I spent the first four years of my life happily in the resort town of Bad Vöslau, close to Vienna. We lived in the very large house my grandparents had acquired more than a century ago to establish my grandfather's medical practice and to have their children, including my father, grow up in a healthy environment, which it provided for me too, years later. My grandfather had died in 1919 and my widowed grandmother, a married aunt and uncle, plus a single aunt and a single uncle, and my parents and I occupied the place. These first few years and subsequent summers in this comfortable setting were my paradise. There I formed the first friendships with my childhood playmates, Lisa and Maria Weissenberg. From playing together in the sandbox until today we—now three widows in America—have maintained a warm relationship. I humorously refer to the large house as our "castle" not merely because of size but also because of the kind of status and security this setting provided us.

When we moved to Vienna my parents rented the lower part of a large villa. There too I had a large garden and playmates, the neighbor's children, Ernst and Ada Sugar, who also became lifelong true and trusted friends. During our early school years, Vienna was slowly recovering from the aftermath of World War I. For a short time, there were economic upswings, construction of public housing projects and health and welfare reforms. Vienna was a cosmopolitan city known as an international model for social democracy. Those years I vividly remember as the carefree time for a child of Viennese Jews, well integrated (or so we thought) in an urban society, made up of a large percentage of respected Jewish business people, professionals, bankers, journalists and politicians. Described as carefree, I tend to forget that as a child I did hear words like revolution, League of Nations, Weimar Republic, Communism, Fascism, Zionism, Yellow Peril and Spanish Civil War; unemployment and depression—words that came up in adult conversations but that I, in my innocence and ignorance, could not understand or define as either good or bad. So complacent was I in my cocoon of just family and then school that all this did not really affect me.

Reflecting on these childhood years, my status within the family always suited me well. For eight years I was an only child that received much attention, not only from my parents, the grandparents Lampl and Grandmother Broessler but also from uncles and aunts. Then, when on July 13, 1931 my sister was born, I became in my own estimation almost an adult. Ruth was for me a living doll to be loved but allowed to be ignored when inconvenient; never that I remember resented. Of my three cousins—Trude (born 1928) and Peter (born 1932) Broessler and Heinz (in America, Henry) Lampl (born 1928) I was the oldest of that generation, treated with respect by Ruth, the cousins and even by our elders. Instinctively I carved out a position of leadership, sensing at the same time that with preferential status also comes responsibility. When I was asked by my parents, uncles and aunts to be in charge of the young ones, I considered this a reasonable duty and not a burden, probably also because these were usually only short-term assignments and only on infrequent occasions. I always had a good feeling for fairness that endeared me to people.

Among my peers in school I was too shy to engage in anything competitive, realizing that there was nothing that made me outstanding. I mingled well and was generally liked by teachers and classmates. Even though not receiving the greatest grades, I seemed to have absorbed what I was taught. The prevailing Austrian school system enabled me to profit throughout life from its basic elementary school, middle school and later forcibly unfinished high school curriculum. Barely fifteen, I was just beginning to read and appreciate good literature, to get interested in the politics of the day, and even to think independently. In those days, dating boys was still somewhat taboo. All the normalcy of my life, including the camaraderie with non-Jewish classmates and my formal education, ended on March 13, 1938, when Hitler annexed Austria. Many in Austria welcomed the German troops, were delighted in the annexation and supported racist Nazi policies, even if many deny this now.

Perhaps it is because of the shock that life had changed forever that I have become so sentimental about the good things that happened before 1938. I still have lasting warm feelings for certain people and places in Austria. Nevertheless, these positive remembrances remain clouded with strong anger toward the regime that so brutally killed millions of people, eradicated noble ideas and robbed so many of the most basic rights of citizenship. Regaining Austrian citizenship has in recent years become an option; probably too late for me now that I have become so deeply rooted in the United States.

In any case, I hope that this introduction to the chapters that follow will in my own words complement Professor Moore's narrative, which he wrote as historian and educator. It is generally known that those who had something to fall back on were better able to cope with adversities. I was fortunate to have grown up in a family that provided enough love for a lifetime. My epilogue will show how this love and the terrible traumatic but also heartwarming experiences that followed the good years shaped my life and enabled me to succeed in the United States from 1947 on.

Eva Broessler Weissman
July 2008
Lakewood, Ohio

Chapter One

Growing Up in Austria

For Austrian Jews, the progression of events that would bring them to the Holocaust began in March 1938 when German troops marched into Austria as the *Anschluss*, or annexation of that country by Nazi Germany, was put into effect. The Nuremberg Laws, which had formalized the anti-Jewish policies of Hitler's regime in 1935, were immediately applied to the Jewish population in Austria. The Anschluss and the Holocaust would prove devastating for Austria's Jews as it did for the entire Jewish population of Europe. At the beginning of 1938, the Jewish population in Austria was around 190,000; by the end of World War II, that number fell to less than 20,000.

One of the 190,000 Jews living in Austria when the Anschluss occurred was Eva Gertrud Broessler. Eva was born in Vienna on September 27, 1923 to Gustav and Thekla Lampl Broessler. Of Austrian descent, the Broessler family could trace its roots back to the eighteenth century.[1] Eva's father, Gustav, was the son of a physician, Dr. Sigmund Broessler, who practiced in Bad Vöslau, a resort town outside of Vienna. Gustav entered the world on July 15, 1891. He was well educated, but neither he nor his three siblings followed their father into medicine. Sigmund did not encourage his children to pursue medical careers. It is possible that Sigmund did not want his children to pursue careers in medicine because the life of a country doctor was a hard one. Despite his father's lack of support, Gustav originally intended to become a doctor, but eventually decided to seek a career outside of medicine. In 1911, after having completed eight years of gymnasium and two more years in *Handelsakadamie*, Gustav turned to the business sector and found employment with the Heinrich Klinger textile firm in Vienna.[2] By the 1930s he had worked his way up to an important management position.[3] Gustav worked as a *Disponent* (materials requirements planner) at Heinrich Klinger, dealing with large buyers, including the City of Vienna and various corporations and mills. His income made him an important source of financial support for his mother, by now a widow, and two sisters. This, along with his poor eyesight, exempted him from serving in the military during World War I. Gustav's interests included family, work, politics, history, medicine, stamp collecting and chess.[4]

Eva's mother, Thekla, was Viennese. Born August 24, 1897, her unusual name was similar to that of a character from a play by Schiller.[5] When Thekla met Gustav she was employed as an executive secretary at the corporate headquarters of the Klinger textile company. Their personal relationship evolved near the end of World War I when Thekla was staying late, working overtime. Gustav had seen the light on in her office, and had deliberately reported it to a security guard who sent Thekla home. This provided Gustav with the opportunity to escort Thekla home, thus beginning their relationship. After they married in 1921, Thekla left the firm and became a full-time housewife as was customary at the time. She shared her husband's interests in politics and voted in elections, paid attention to current events, and liked to read.[6] Thekla was by no means what Americans today would consider a typical "European housewife going to the market in her babushka," Eva insists. She was a fine cook, entertained family members at dinners, supervised and trained the household help and took care of her household "in each and every way." Thekla did beautiful needlework, cross stitching, embroidery and knitting, although her preference was for crocheting.[7]

The Austria into which Eva was born was only a sliver of what it had been a decade earlier. Austria had been carved out of the old Austro-Hungarian Empire by the Treaty of Saint-Germain-en-Laye after the end of World War I, with Hungary, Czechoslovakia and the Kingdom of Serbs, Croats and Slovenes having been declared independent states, and other portions of the Empire's former territories having been divided among Italy, Poland and Yugoslavia. The treaty limited the size of the Austrian army and required the payment of reparations to the victorious allied powers. It also prohibited the joining of Austria with Germany, although the majority of Austrians probably would have preferred to have their country become part of Germany.[8]

Generally speaking, the postwar years in Austria had been less tumultuous than they were in Germany, and the country seemed to be fully recovering from the conflict. Following an early struggle with inflation and influenza, Austria appeared to settle into a period of relative stability. The fact that Austria's political situation was less complex than Germany's at this time also contributed to this state of affairs. The two parties that emerged during this time, the Social Democrats and Christian Democrats, dominated the political scene for the most part. The two-party system in Austria split the nation, however, as their differences reflected not only the normal disparity between conservatives and liberals but also exacerbated the contradictions between two very different elements of Austrian society that were now forced to live together. One of these elements was the city of Vienna, in which twenty-five percent of Austria's population resided. Once the imperial capital of the Austro-Hungarian Empire, Vienna was a cosmopolitan, freethinking and industrialized area with a large number of Slavic and Jewish inhabitants, who routinely supported the Social Democratic Party. Making up the rest of the new Austrian state were provinces torn from the old Danubian and Alpine regions of the empire. These provinces were largely rural, conservative, Catholic, mistrustful of foreigners and a likely source of anti-Semitism. Politically, they leaned toward the Christian Socialists, a Catholic party with a history of reform that would embrace more authoritarian politics late in the 1920s. The two political parties managed to co-exist, although they did so uneasily, throughout the twenties. The Christian Socialists controlled the federal government and the rural provinces, while the Social Democrats dominated Vienna, which was set up as an independent province under the terms of the St. Germain treaty.[9]

The Social Democrats came into power in Vienna following World War I; they had brought an end to anti-Semitic riots that had occurred earlier, and under their leadership Vienna's economy was beginning to enjoy significant prosperity. The party's leaders, Karl Seitz, Karl Renner, Dr. Julius Deutsch, and Otto Bauer, were perceived by many as progressive and sincere democrats whose goals were to restore order to the country and improve the lives of its people. Hospitals, kindergartens, and parks were constructed; housing shortages were attacked by building modern housing projects for the workers. Tax increases on industries, entertainment and luxury items funded these programs. Not everyone found the new tax laws acceptable, however. The Christian Socialist Party, whose appeal was to the clergy, industrialists, and peasants, opposed the tax policies of the Social Democrats and campaigned against them. In 1921, the Christian Socialists pushed the Separation Act through the legislature. This law cut the ties between Vienna and the lower Austrian provinces. It was after this that Vienna became an internationally recognized model for socialism and the programs noted above were implemented.[10]

In addition, both parties built up their own paramilitary groups in the 1920s. The Social Democrats created a group that they labeled the people's militia (*Volkswehr*), while the Christian Socialists organized an opposing army of supporters who called themselves the Home Defense (*Heimwehr*). There was also an active Communist Party, but it was perceived as being no real threat to the major political parties, and it was generally thought that the rivalry between the Christian Socialists and Social Democrats was unlikely to threaten Austria's tranquility or prosperity.[11]

Like Germany after the war, Austria suffered from significant economic problems, especially from rampant inflation. Paper money was printed in larger and larger denominations, and the value of the paper currency (*Notgeld*) dropped precipitously over the immediate postwar years until it was virtually worthless. Thekla had saved money with which she hoped to buy her future household goods, but after the war those savings were barely enough to buy a pair of patent leather shoes. Gustav traded stamps to earn extra money, taking advantage of the fact that stamps still had some value while paper money was worthless. Despite the hyperinflationary times, however, Gustav and Thekla married and moved into the Broessler home in Bad Vöslau.

Eva never knew her paternal grandfather, due to his untimely demise in 1919, but she spent the first four years of her life and summer vacations at the home of her paternal grandmother in Bad Vöslau. The home was large and Eva had plenty of room to play. Eva had an ideal place to enjoy the earliest years of her life. Bad Vöslau has been described as a beautiful resort community that was ideally suited for families with small children. There were two public swimming pools where mineral water flowed continuously from a spring, music could be heard in the park during the afternoons, and the community was surrounded by woods where one could walk and enjoy the scent of pine trees.[12]

In 1927, the family moved to Vienna permanently, although the Broesslers continued to spend their summer vacations in Bad Vöslau. The "roaring twenties" had been an exciting time in the city, reflected in the exuberant postwar atmosphere that existed and in the city's nightlife. But there was an undercurrent of tension building in Vienna. On July 15, 1927, Vienna was rocked by the Ringstrasse Demonstration, which became violent, with police firing shots at the demonstrators. The Social and Christian Democrats blamed each other for the violence, but the real source of the trouble was a violently anti-Semitic group known as the "Swastika Men" (*Hakenkreuzler*), the forerunner of the Nazi Party in Austria. (The Christian Socialists tended to tolerate the Hakenkreuzler since they opposed both Jews and the Social Democrats.)

The July demonstration may have been a reaction to an earlier incident in January 1927 at Schattendorf, near Vienna, where a Hakenkreuzler shooting spree brought about the deaths of two people, one a child, and the wounding of several others. Three men had confessed to firing the fatal shots, but they were acquitted at their trial. The unjustness of the verdict outraged the working classes, and their anger seems to have festered until the outbreak of violence in July. By now the Social Democrats had reached the zenith of their power; from this point onward the party seems to have gone into a slow decline with fascism gradually gaining in popularity.[13]

In Vienna, the Broesslers settled into an apartment located at Severin Schreibergasse 1, Wien XVIII, in a suburban area of the city. They lived next door to Endre and Jenny Sugar, whose two children, Ernst and Ada, became Eva's closest childhood friends. The three would spend hours playing in the garden that connected their homes. When they turned five, Eva and Ada began to attend kindergarten. Doing so was not obligatory, and children who attended usually came from families who could afford to send their children there. Eva liked kindergarten, but after an occasion when the class took a trip to a nearby park, an altercation with the teacher led Eva to stop attending. Eva had wandered away from the group a short distance, and the teacher frightened her by stating that the police would come if Eva did not return to the group immediately.[14]

Later on, in elementary school, Eva and Ada shared a bench with Hansi Engl, thus beginning a lifelong friendship that the three girls would come to call their "everlasting triumvirate."[15] Like Eva, Hansi and Ada survived the war. Hansi and her parents escaped Austria and made their way to England. There Hansi was trained in psychoanalysis by Anna Freud and eventually succeeded her as co-director of the Hempstead Child Therapy Clinic in London, after Freud's death. Hansi died in 2003. Ada and her parents escaped to Venezuela; Ada became a teacher and currently lives in Milan with her husband Arnold Rink. Her brother Ernst became a geologist and an oil company executive.[16] They came to know each other's families well, and the impact of the Holocaust undoubtedly helped sustain their friendship over the years. Eva is also very much aware of the importance of the Holocaust on the lives of the Sugar family, and the continuation of their close relationship. She has remarked that "really perhaps the friendship wouldn't have been that intimate or that everlasting had it not been for Hitler."[17] Now she is extremely glad it blossomed.

Eva attended elementary school between the ages of six and ten before progressing to a semi-private gymnasium, which she would have attended until she was eighteen, had events not interrupted her education when she was fifteen. In fact, Eva never finished her formal education, although she would have liked to.[18] She described herself as being "interested" in knowing, but she was not an outstanding student. She was typical of her generation in that she held to the common view that women were expected to marry and have children. Although she had some "intellectual ideas" back then, Eva tended to share the belief of her friends and society in general that she would marry and raise a family.[19] In looking back on those days, however, Eva is not certain that she would necessarily have done so without having first learned a trade or profession.

The Vienna that Eva moved to in 1927 was a sophisticated and cultured city. Eva grew up in an era of social democracy in Vienna and she saw some of the best of those years. To some degree, even with the violence of January and July, Vienna seemed to have entered an age of reform when Eva began her schooling. There was a good health care system, quality childcare, excellent baby clinics, and first-rate public education. Schools provided free meals and milk to their students, a progressive innovation at that time. Eva recalls that a decline in social services began when the Christian Democrats replaced the Social Democratic Party as the majority party in the government, and the government "got worse even before Hitler."[20]

A thriving Jewish community existed in Vienna. As in some other countries, Jews were required to register with the *Israelitsche Kultusgemeinde*, an agency authorized by the government to issue documents relating to vital statistics, such as birth, death, and marriage certificates.[21] The home Eva and her family lived in was not in a "Jewish" neighborhood, and her neighbors included Christian and Jewish families. Vienna's population did include Jews who had immigrated from Eastern Europe, but native Viennese Jews did not always associate with them, as differences in culture, language, and economics often kept the native and immigrant Jewish populations separate from each other. Eva recalls a sense of embarrassment about dealing with the non-Viennese Jews as they lacked the education or money the native Jewish population had, and they did not speak German well, if at all. Eva thinks now, however, that those feelings reflected some of her own prejudices and were not necessarily typical of the times.[22]

Vienna had begun to attract Jewish residents in the middle of the twelfth century. By 1623, Jews were banned from the inner city. For a time afterwards, they were confined to ghettos and then, in 1670, they were ordered out of the city by Emperor Leopold I. Eventually Leopold, for economic reasons, asked them to return. Official discrimination against Jews in Vienna continued for another two centuries until they were granted full civil rights in 1867, well after many other European states had extended such freedoms to their Jewish populations. The new laws permitted Jews to own property in Vienna, to serve in the government, and to have greater access to universities. The result of this legislation was to bring about a wave of immigration that caused Vienna's Jewish population to swell from about 6,000 in 1860 to more than 175,000 in 1910 (nearly nine percent of the city's total population). Especially attractive to Vienna's Jews was the opportunity to acquire an education; by about 1900 roughly a third of the university students in Vienna were Jewish, a significant percentage of whom were studying medicine or law. Comparable levels of success were noted in business and the arts. By the end of the nineteenth century, fifty percent of the banks in Austria were Jewish-owned and Jews held eighty percent of the key positions in the banking world. In Vienna, Jews played a significant role in the newspaper industry as publishers, editors and contributors. The London *Times* would report by the turn of the century that Jews were at the forefront economically, politically, and in terms of influence throughout Austria.[23]

Not everyone in Vienna appreciated the success of the city's Jewish population. The gains that Jews had made often led to unwanted competition with Gentiles, and non-Jews who felt they were being hurt or displaced by these successes were resentful. Moreover, underlying anti-Semitic feelings in Vienna were intensified by the fear that poor Jews from Russia and Eastern Europe, seeking refuge from the pogroms taking place there, might overwhelm Vienna with an entirely alien Jewish presence.[24] And so, despite what appear to be Eva's generally positive memories of childhood in Vienna, it is clear that by 1927, an undercurrent of anti-Jewish sentiment did exist in the city and was beginning to make itself felt. In the 1930s, Austrian anti-Semitism would increase in intensity.

Although Eva's grandfather had belonged to a small Jewish prayer house and was chairman of the board there, her immediate family was casual about their religion. They did not observe the fast days, for instance, and Gustav was not strict about going to the synagogue to worship. For a time, Gustav seems to have been something of a freethinker, questioning the need for religion in that "modern" age—a not uncommon view for Jews in Vienna at that time. Even so, Eva was encouraged to attend youth services at synagogue on Saturdays. The family did not belong to any particular synagogue, but did attend services occasionally and celebrated Passover from time to time. Despite their informal religious observations, the Broesslers were "keenly" aware of their Jewishness, and had a cultural identification as such. A few family members married non-Jews, but most who did so did not convert. The majority of the family's friends were Jewish, although some of them were also in mixed marriages with non-Jews.[25]

Religion was a required course of study in public school, and Eva recalls that it was generally known in school who was Jewish and who was not. Religion classes were held separately for Catholics and Jews; very few Protestants (who would have been Lutherans) attended Eva's school. She can recall only one Lutheran student in her class. Eva thought her religion teachers were excellent, and she learned some Hebrew so that she could read prayers. Despite the separate classes in religious studies, Eva has no personal recollections of anti-Semitism from her school days.[26]

Eva was exposed to Catholicism to a greater degree than many of her friends might have been. This largely came about as a result of the birth of Eva's sister Ruth on July 13, 1931. The long-standing family joke was that Ruth was delivered by zeppelin, rather than by the stork. This was because the Sugar family had included Eva in a trip to see a zeppelin landing in Vienna on the day before Ruth was born. After Ruth's birth, the Broesslers hired a Catholic woman named Mitzi (Maria) Ponlechner to do housework and to care for the infant. Out of respect for Mitzi's faith the Broesslers observed the then traditional Catholic practice of eating fish on Fridays. Ruth occasionally attended Mass with Mitzi, and Eva was also made aware of some aspects of Catholicism. She is glad to have been exposed to another faith, and can still recite the Lord's Prayer in German.[27]

By the time Ruth was born, conditions in Austria were beginning to change for the worse. Vienna was now in the grip of the Great Depression, and, as happened throughout Europe and the United States, people saw their savings wiped out due to bank collapses or falling stock prices; unemployment increased as well. Yet the Viennese economy recovered from the Depression more quickly than many other European cities. Some thought that life in Vienna before Hitler was an easy one, so easy that most middle-class families could afford to hire at least one maid. As a result, although this was not always so, many housewives began to enjoy more leisurely lives as servants assumed the responsibility of caring for the home and children, although this was not entirely the case in the Broessler household.[28]

The impact of the Great Depression was, of course, felt by the Broesslers. Her father's income, like that of so many during these times, had dropped and this meant that Eva and her family had to move to a new, less expensive, flat. Even renting a more modest apartment strained the family's resources. The Broessler's new home was at Gersthoferstrasse 28, still in the Eighteenth District of Vienna, where their first apartment was located. The new apartment was in a more economically mixed neighborhood than the one on Severin Schreibergasse, which was indicative of a step down socially. Eva and her family now resided in a building that had stores occupying the ground floor. There was no garden like the one Eva and her friends had played in before, although there was a park a few blocks away. Nor was there a telephone in the flat. Gustav would either have to make calls from his office, or he would have to use a telephone booth on the street. Messages could also be sent fairly quickly by pneumatic mail (the *Rohrpost*), usually arriving within a few hours from one district to another. There were positive aspects to the move, however. Their new flat had better plumbing and a heated bathroom. Also, the apartment was located on a streetcar line so that Gustav's commuting time to work was reduced.

When they moved to Vienna permanently in 1927, Gustav and Thekla engaged the services of Rosi Achatz to assist with the housework, and she and the family became very close. When Mitzi Ponlechner joined the family as Ruth's nanny, she, too, developed a close relationship with the family. Even during their reduced circumstances in the Depression years, the family was able to retain the services of both full-time and part-time household help. Both women would correspond with the family for years after they emigrated from Austria, and Mitzi would later play a critical role in the lives of Gustav and Thekla.

Gustav usually came home from work for the midday repast, which was the main meal of the day in most middle-class households. This typically consisted of three courses: soup, a meat and vegetable dish, and dessert. Evening meals were much lighter, often just cold cuts or, perhaps, a casserole. A good deal of socializing took place with family. Thekla had two younger brothers, Max and Felix, who were both married. Gustav had a brother, Otto, who was married, and two sisters, Jetti (Henriette) and Grete. Major holidays and birthdays were celebrated with the entire family, where Eva and her sister, parents, cousins, aunts and uncles and grandparents would share in the festive occasions.[29]

Summer vacations were usually spent in Bad Vöslau, at the home of Eva's paternal grandparents. Although Sigmund had died in 1919 before Eva was born, his widow, Berta, continued to live in the eighteen-room house. Although she rented out part of the house to others, the heavily mortgaged estate was never fully occupied and Berta struggled to keep the property. Gustav and his brother pleaded with her to sell the house, but Berta preferred to stay and to tend the garden that she loved so much. Gustav's sister, Grete, and her husband lived in the house and continued to do so after Eva and her parents moved out.

The Great Depression was just one shadow that was beginning to spread over Austria. The tension between the Social Democrats and Christian Socialists was escalating, as the violence of 1927 demonstrated. By 1929, the Christian Socialists were pushing for a more authoritarian governmental structure and by the next year their paramilitary groups were attracting secret assistance from Mussolini's Italy. The onset of the Great Depression in 1931 only served to further exacerbate the division between the two parties and helped to bring about a period of increasing authoritarianism.[30]

At the same time, the Nazi Party was growing, both in numbers and influence, and the Nazis' anti-Jewish propaganda was becoming increasingly venomous as their popularity increased. Nor was anti-Semitic propaganda the only thing that was on the upswing; violence against Jews was also becoming more common. The Hakenkreuzler were expanding their attacks upon

Jews, carrying out what were essentially terrorist actions against Vienna's Jewish population. Jewish business establishments and theaters were attacked with stink bombs, while Jewish cemeteries were vandalized. There were physical attacks by brown-shirted Nazis as well. The activities of the Hakenkreuzler were not always endured with forbearance. Some Jews fought back when they were attacked by Hakenkreuzler thugs, and Jewish youth groups mobilized to guard the streets and cemeteries.[31]

Despite the anti-Jewish diatribes and slogans and the danger of physical harm, the Austrian people as a whole and the Jews in particular seem to have been slow to recognize the rising tide of fascism. The prevailing sense was that as long as order prevailed, it would continue to do so and that the good life that existed in Vienna would not come to an end. In the early 1930s, the Hakenkreuzler were regarded by most Austrians, including many Jews, as an insignificant nuisance. Some small outbreaks of anti-Semitism were not uncommon, after all, and few, if any, anticipated that events such as these would evolve into something much worse.[32]

The ascension of Adolf Hitler to power in Germany in 1933 served as an indication of things to come. In 1934, German Jews began to face new sets of restrictions on their lives. Gradually Viennese Jews learned of the anti-Jewish activities taking place in Germany, and a few at least felt that the events that were occurring under Hitler's regime were just a forerunner of things to come. Yet most Austrian Jews found it difficult to believe that such discrimination could occur in their homeland or that the Austrian government would ever go so far as to submit to a Nazi takeover of the nation.[33]

Not everyone was sanguine about the future. Some began to prepare for the worst by arranging to protect their businesses should the Nazis ever intervene in Austrian affairs, or take control of the country. A common method of doing so was to arrange for a Gentile to accept nominal ownership of a business enterprise, which would allow the firm's true Jewish proprietor to maintain an income from the business. Despite these types of precautions, however, the majority of Vienna's Jews failed "to recognize the danger signs for what they were;" after the war survivors would marvel "at our blindness at [the German] approach." Put simply, most of the Jewish population of Austria could not comprehend that the way of life they were enjoying, and which seemed likely to go on indefinitely, could ever come to an end. Furthermore, while Nazi propaganda was spreading and beginning to appear more and more openly, the insidious process took place gradually so that most Jews in Vienna continued to live as they had always done.[34]

The political situation in Austria began to deteriorate in 1933. Englebert Dollfuss, a Christian Socialist, had come to power the previous year. Quickly discerning that he could not govern within the original constitutional framework, and reacting to Hitler's rise to power in Germany, Dollfuss resorted to authoritarianism. In March 1933, Dollfuss dissolved all parliamentary activities and then ordered the dissolution of the Nazi and Socialist Democratic parties. The decree soon brought about a confrontation between the Socialists and Christian Democrats. A battle between the paramilitary troops of the two parties erupted in Vienna in February 1934, leaving hundreds dead and wounded. The fighting eventually resulted in the defeat of the Social Democrats and broke the party's power.[35]

Dollfuss' policy ultimately failed. Had the Christian Socialists and Social Democrats put their differences aside and worked together to defeat the Nazis, they might have delayed the growth of that party's influence in Austria, although it is likely that they would have only postponed the country's absorption by Hitler's Germany. The prohibition of Nazism in Austria had little effect. While it may have been against the law to be a Nazi in Austria after the Christian Socialists took control, the Nazi Party continued to thrive in Austria and to exploit a latent background of anti-Semitism there. As the Nazis campaigned against Dollfuss, they continually railed against the Jewish domination of the Chancellor. In time, the Nazis would vow to seize and redistribute Jewish property in Austria. By the summer of 1934, despite their prohibition, the Austrian Nazis felt they had grown strong enough to take over the country. The attempt took place on July 25, and, although the *putsch* failed, it did result in the death of Chancellor Dollfuss.[36] The Nazi coup was foiled in part because Mussolini moved troops into the Brenner Pass and declared that Italy would guard Austrian independence.

Dollfuss was succeeded by Kurt von Schuschnigg and the new chancellor soon demonstrated his resolve to assert the government's authority. Schuschnigg upheld the authoritarian constitution that had been voted into effect three months before his predecessor's assassination. Now a single party, the Fatherland Front (which had absorbed most of the Christian Socialist Party), dominated the scene under what became known as the *Ständestaat*, a sort of clerical-fascist regime. Schuschnigg would manage to keep Austria out of German hands for nearly four years. Inside Austria little seemed to have changed; the government may have become a dictatorship, but its rule was not harsh and life seemed to go on normally. The Nazis, however, continued to prepare for the day when Germany's annexation of Austria would become a reality. The Social Democrats remained unreconciled, and the Fatherland Front drew its support from a narrow base of clericalism and conservatives. Only the pledge of Italian support maintained Schuschnigg in power, and, when Mussolini began to drift closer to Nazi Germany in 1936, the days of Austrian independence were numbered.[37] The lives of all Austrians were about to undergo a dramatic change; for Austria's Jews the future was about to become a nightmare of unimaginable terror.

NOTES

1. Eva G. Weissman, *A Life With a View*, unpublished memoir (hereafter *Life*).
2. Correspondence between Eva Broessler Weissman and Gregory Moore, August 25, 2005.
3. Eva G. Weissman, *Shoah*, USC Shoah Foundation Institute for Visual History and Education, Copy of videotape on file in the Tolerance Resource Center, Notre Dame College, South Euclid, Ohio (hereafter *Shoah*).
4. Ibid.
5. Ibid.
6. Ibid.
7. Weissman to Moore, August 25, 2005.
8. Roland N. Stromberg, *Europe in the Twentieth Century*, Third edition (Englewood Cliffs, N.J.: Prentice Hall, 1992), 120.
9. James Wilkinson and H. Stuart Hughes, *Contemporary Europe: A History*, Ninth edition (Upper Saddle River, N.J.: Prentice Hall, 1998), 206–207.
10. Vienna Webservice, http://www.wien.gv.at; Helen Hilsenrad, *Brown Was the Danube* (New York: Thomas Yoseloff, 1966), 125–126.
11. Ibid.
12. Hilsenrad, 161.
13. Hilsenrad, 162–164.
14. Marilyn Harran, Dieter Kuntz, et al., *The Holocaust Chronicle* (Lakewood, Illinois: Publications International, Ltd., 2003) (hereafter HC); Weissman to Moore, August 25, 2005.
15. Ibid.
16. Ernst died in 2004.
17. Weissman, *Shoah*; HC.
18. Ibid.
19. Ibid.
20. Ibid.
21. Ibid.
22. Ibid.
23. HC, 29; Friedländer, Saul, *Nazi Germany and the Jews: The Years of Persecution, 1933–1939* (New York: HarperCollins, 1997), 80.
24. Ibid.
25. Weissman, *Shoah*; HC; Ruth Newmark, *Shoah*, USC Shoah Foundation Institute for Visual History and Education, Copy of videotape on file in the Tolerance Resource Center, Notre Dame College, South Euclid, Ohio (hereafter Newmark, *Shoah*).
26. Weissman, *Shoah*; Weissman, *Life*.

27. Weissman, *Life*.
28. Hilsenrad, 191, 195.
29. Ruth Newmark, unpublished memoir (2006), 3–11 (hereafter *Memoir*).
30. Wilkinson and Hughes, 207.
31. Hilsenrad, 202–203.
32. Hilsenrad, 202–203, 164–166.
33. Ibid.
34. Hilsenrad, 205–206.
35. Wilkinson and Hughes, 238–239.
36. Wilkinson and Hughes, 238–239; Hilsenrad, 220–221; HC, 82; Friedländer, *Nazi Germany and the Jews*, 242; Vienna Webservice, http://www.wien.gv.at
37. Wilkinson and Hughes, 239; Vienna Webservice, http://www.wien.gv.at

Chapter Two

From Austria to The Netherlands

Adolf Hitler came to power in Germany on January 30, 1933. Eva, who was a few months past her ninth birthday, heard her parents and others speak of Hitler. Family members and others felt that "a lunatic like Hitler won't last forever." There were no immediate changes in Austria as Hitler consolidated his rule in Germany, but as noted in Chapter One, anti-Semitism became more overt there in the 1930s.

The Broesslers had always been aware of some level of anti-Semitism in Austria. Before the rise of Hitler, Austrian anti-Semitism seemed more abstract; people might express their dislike of Jews in general, but didn't necessarily apply that attitude in personal relationships. Eva certainly didn't feel any less for being Jewish; it was a part of her and she never thought that it would be better not to be Jewish. She heard some people refer to Jews with epithets such as "pigs" but Eva simply felt such individuals were "crazy." In general, she felt secure in her family and anti-Semites were considered to be harmless.[1]

Even with how the Austrians would eventually act toward Jews, Eva feels she enjoyed a happy childhood and she has many good memories and feelings. Her sister Ruth, who was eight years younger, feels differently, however, since her childhood coincided almost entirely with increasing anti-Semitism.[2] Nonetheless, the growing influence of the Nazis in Austria throughout the 1930s concerned the Broessler family very much. By 1937, although it was still technically illegal to be a Nazi in Austria, the movement was clearly growing and was becoming more brazen in its activities. Large swastikas could be seen painted on walls, and anti-Jewish slogans or signs were appearing on Jewish-owned shops and businesses. Jewish shopkeepers were beginning to notice that Gentiles were avoiding their businesses. But Jews could still walk the streets of Vienna freely. Nazism, however, was beginning to develop a cult-like status in Austria and the anti-Semitic feelings that had always lurked beneath the surface of Viennese and Austrian society were beginning to manifest themselves more openly.[3]

It was hard to believe that there could be such a turn in people's feelings for Austria's Jewish population. Anti-Semitism was not thought of as a national characteristic of Austria by many, and there was a failure to recognize the danger signs for what they were. A resident of Vienna at that time, Helen Hilsenrad, has written that "we simply could not get it through our heads that an abrupt halt could come to a way of life which was good and which seemed continuous."[4]

Life for Eva and Ruth and their parents, as well as for all of Austria's Jewish population, changed forever in March 1938 when the Anschluss, Germany's annexation of Austria, was announced. Still a few months shy of her fifteenth birthday, Eva heard the news of the annexation on the radio. There had been stories that the Austrian Prime Minister, Kurt von Schuschnigg, had gone to Germany to talk to Hitler, and there was a sense among many that the Anschluss could be avoided. But it happened, nevertheless.[5]

There was little resistance when the Germans marched into Austria, but Eva sensed that what was happening was bad, although she had no knowledge, nor did anyone else, of the beginnings of Hitler's "Final Solution" regarding Europe's Jews. Her sister, Ruth, remembered that the streets became fearful as many Austrians celebrated the annexation. Nazi flags were everywhere and people began using the stiff-armed Nazi salute.

Eva recalls that Cardinal Theodor Innitzer of Vienna met with Hitler after his arrival in Vienna, but she is uncertain whether or not he did so in the name of peace. She does know that the Cardinal aided the daughter of the chief rabbi of Vienna, Edith Taglicht, who had been one of Eva's religion teachers, in her escape from Berlin before the war began.[6]

The Anschluss brought swift, dramatic, and harsh changes in the lives of Austria's Jewish population. Young and old alike, Jews were taken from their shops and homes immediately after the Nazi occupation and publicly humiliated. A common form of humiliation was to force Jews to clean the streets. Jewish families began to keep in closer touch, spreading word of new humiliations and acts of violence. The treatment of Jews could be random as well. Caught in a general roundup, a Jew might be surprised to find himself being released because a friend or former schoolmate recognized him and let him go. The persecution continued relentlessly, however, so that an atmosphere of loathing toward Jews was being created. Anti-Semitic threats and slogans were smeared on Jewish stores, and Jewish store owners might be degraded by being forced to wear signs that read "I am a dirty Jew. Don't buy at this store." Other Jews were forced to carry similar signs through Vienna's streets for the amusement of the non-Jewish population.

The violence in the first week after the Anschluss was so great that the Gestapo[7] was ordered to crack down on the excesses. Few Nazis heeded the orders, instead blaming the violence on Communists, which set off a new round of violence. Ultimately it took a threat of reductions in rank for SA[8] leaders whose men took part in the excesses to curb the violence to some degree. Jews were forced to remove posters supporting opponents of the Nazis in the elections that were supposed to (but did not) take place after the annexation. Jews continued to be ridiculed on the streets, and Jews were prohibited from attending movies or concerts and could not use the public parks and swimming pools.[9]

Even worse, arrests and deportations to concentration camps such as Dachau[10] began; the father of one of Eva's school friends was one of the first to die there.[11] Eva was touched and moved to learn of a relative, Steffi Ungar, who, in order to protect her young children from the knowledge that their father had been sent to Dachau, stayed up at night writing letters to them and signing them with their father's name, as if he were away on an extended trip.[12] In fact, the policy of the Nazis after the Anschluss was to make life in Austria so unpleasant for Jews that they would emigrate. Under the direction of Adolf Eichmann, the reign of terror that was implemented was designed to make Austrian Jews eager to leave. Jews were systematically stripped of their property, businesses, bank accounts and legal rights. Within six months of his assignment to Austria, Eichmann's system had resulted in the emigration of almost 45,000 Austrian Jews. By May 1939, about 100,000 of the 190,000 Jews in Austria had left the country.[13]

The new policies toward Jews naturally impacted upon the Broessler family. Their family home, in Bad Vöslau, a house with eighteen rooms and what Ruth describes as a "beautiful garden," was deeded over to Eva's aunt, Maria Broessler, who was not Jewish. This was done in order to avoid having the house confiscated by the Nazis. In Vienna, Eva and her family were still living in their apartment on Gersthoferstrasse. The family's bank accounts and insurance policies were confiscated, however, and they were made to take their valuables to Gestapo headquarters.[14] In effect, the Broessler family, as did all Jews in Austria, lost its identity and place in society. Now it was as if they did not belong any more. As Ruth would say later: "Day and night we were not sure of our life."[15] The measures imposed by the Nazis following the Anschluss served to separate the Austrian Jews from the social mainstream of their country and targeted them for additional persecution, as they relentlessly stepped up the pressure to drive them from the country. The pressures and misery were so great in the first weeks of the Anschluss that the number of

Jewish suicides in Austria multiplied by twenty times between February and March 1938, from four in February to seventy-nine in March.[16]

The Broesslers did not escape the increased restrictions upon their lives. The girls could no longer associate with their non-Jewish friends, for one thing, and had to attend a separate school for Jews. One day, at their new school, a photographer from an anti-Semitic newspaper came to photograph children who were representative of what stereotypically were considered to be "Jewish" physiques. Eva remembers her sister coming home from school that day crying because the photographer had not selected her, and not understanding the reason why. "The photographer did not take me," Ruth sobbed.[17]

In June 1938, the Jewish-owned textile firm Gustav worked for was "Aryanized." To be Aryanized meant that Jews could no longer own or run businesses or industries. Through the Property Transfer Office (*Vermögensverkehrsstelle*), which had been established in mid-May, Jewish economic assets were being placed under "Aryan" ownership or supervision. Additionally, Jews were no longer permitted to work for Aryan companies. After more than twenty-seven years with Heinrich Klinger, Gustav was fired. Soon after, the Broesslers were evicted from their apartment on Gersthoferstrasse and they had to move in with relatives in another district in Vienna. Their new home was located at Stumpergasse 2 in Mariahilf, Vienna's Sixth District. Here the family stayed in the small flat Thekla's widowed Aunt Anna shared with her blind brother Ludwig.[18]

Despite the growing persecution of Jews and the obvious desire on the part of the Nazis to drive them from Austria, the Broesslers, like so many Jewish families in both Germany and Austria, did not give much thought to leaving their homeland. They were afraid, of course, as the Nazi policies made life more and more dangerous for them, but as Eva noted, the family had no immediate plans to emigrate. Part of the reason for this was the notion that they had nowhere to go; they couldn't just leave their homeland. There was also a certain naiveté involved, a sense of "where would we go?" Nor did the family have extensive resources. Unlike some families, the Broesslers did not have a Swiss bank account or other assets that the Nazis would have been unable to touch.[19]

Had the Broessler family decided to find a way out of Austria in the first months of the Anschluss, they would have been hampered by the closing of the Israelitsche Kultusgemeinde, which would have been the agency through which they would have made arrangements to leave. Its officials were shipped off to Dachau, thereby depriving Vienna's Jews of an important source of support. In May, however, with the policy of forced emigration of Austria's Jews fully underway, the Kultusgemeinde re-opened under the watchful eye of the Nazis, and assumed responsibility for both emigration and social aid.[20] Later, in order to make the process of driving the Jewish population out of the country more efficient, the Germans created the Central Office for Jewish Emigration (*Zentralstelle für Jüdische Auswanderung*) in August. This was done to overcome a lack of coordination between the various agencies that had to process the documents necessary to obtain authorization to leave Austria. The Central Office also extorted fees from wealthy Jews seeking to emigrate and used those funds to finance the emigration of poorer Jews.[21]

The events of *Kristallnacht*, November 10, 1938, changed everything. On that terrifying night, as mobs in Germany and Austria rampaged through the streets, Gustav Broessler was arrested. That day, German authorities arrived at the Broessler apartment and demanded to enter their flat. During a search of the apartment, they removed a number of banned books (written by Jewish authors), seized some valuables, and searched for other "dangerous" items. Gustav was arrested, apparently for no other reason than that he was Jewish. He was taken off to a nearby holding facility where he was kept most of the day.[22]

Thekla acted swiftly. Somehow she discovered where Gustav and the other Jewish men who had been abducted were being held. Contacting a local official, she learned that if she could provide proof that her husband was not fit for physical labor, he could be released. Dashing home, Thekla went through the family's papers and found the documents that had exempted Gustav for military service during World War I. She presented these to the bureaucrat and he released Gustav.

While Thekla was arranging for Gustav's release, help came from an unexpected quarter. Gustav's brother Otto was married to a Catholic named Maria, Eva's "Aunt Mitzi." When she heard about her brother-in-law's detainment, Maria contacted an influential person she knew in an effort to win Gustav's freedom. While Thekla was out, Maria arrived at their apartment with this individual, a military officer. When they knocked on the door of the apartment, Eva, who had been left in charge of her young sister, came to the door and looked through the glass peephole; all she could see was a man in a military uniform. She was so frightened that it took some effort to convince her that she and Ruth were in no danger and to finally allow her aunt and the officer in. Their offer of aid proved to be unnecessary. Thekla and Gustav returned soon after, to the relief and joy of them all. It had now become clear to the family that they could no longer remain in Austria as it was becoming far too dangerous for Jews. Indeed, if Thekla had not acted so quickly, Gustav almost certainly would have been on his way to Dachau.[23]

The next few days vividly imprinted the full scope of Kristallnacht on Eva and the rest of the family. They learned that some 6,000 Viennese Jewish men had been rounded up and arrested simply because they were Jews. Most had been shipped off to concentration camps, and the Broesslers realized how fortunate they were that Eva's father had been spared that fate. They could see the results of the violence for themselves: burned and looted synagogues, Jewish institutions vandalized and Jewish-owned stores with broken windows that had been pillaged and defaced with anti-Semitic slogans. They could hear the cheering of crowds of onlookers as the violence took place, and they were aware that the authorities had done nothing to curb the rioting. The final indignity was that Jewish associations in Vienna were being fined in order to pay for the damage that had been done.

Gustav had a Hungarian-born cousin in the United States, Dr. Franz Alexander, a prominent psychoanalyst and founder of the Psychoanalytic Institute of Chicago. Alexander had many siblings. One of them, Magda, who was an art historian, had married a psychologist and had moved with him from Budapest to Amsterdam, while another sister, Borka Rényi, still lived in Budapest. She had visited the Broesslers in early 1938, and advised them at that time to leave Vienna. Gustav had told her he didn't know how the family could possibly do so. But now, after his narrow escape, Gustav was convinced that the family would have to find a way out of Austria in order to ensure their safety.

Getting out of Austria was not a simple matter. In order to leave the country, persons had to be able to prove they had a place to go, which meant getting affidavits of support from friends or family members from the countries to which they hoped to emigrate. Additionally, they would have to find the money to pay a steep emigration tax. Fortunately, Borka had already taken the liberty of writing to her brother and sisters who were living abroad, seeking the necessary affidavits for the Broesslers so that they could leave Austria for the United States. Gustav, meanwhile, went to the American consulate in order to apply for a visa, only to discover that the quotas for Austrian immigration, which had been low to begin with, had been filled for 1938, meaning they would not be able to apply for entry into the United States until 1939. Efforts to obtain visas for Cuba, China, and Portugal also failed.[24]

Entry into the United States for European Jews was difficult under the best of circumstances in 1938. Not only were there quota restrictions, but anti-Semitism and a general suspicion of immigrants added to the problem. (The problem remained throughout the decade. For example, in June 1940, an additional obstacle for immigrants seeking entry into the United States appeared. Fearing that some immigrants might actually be spies or saboteurs, Third Assistant Secretary of State Breckenridge Long implemented a restrictive policy regarding the issuing of visas to prospective immigrants. While some perceived Long's policy as hostile to foreigners in general and Jewish refugees in particular, Long defended his action on national security grounds.)[25]

The effort to obtain a visa to the United States was not without hope. Dr. Alexander had responded to Borka's request, and air mailed the required affidavits of support for the Broessler family. There were so many difficulties to overcome in Vienna in regard to getting visas for the entire family, however, that Gustav and Thekla decided that it would be best to move Eva and Ruth to The Netherlands in order to get the two girls to a safe haven as soon as possible. The family connection to the Alexanders made the Dutch option seem advisable. The psychologist that Magda had married, Géza Révész, was also Hungarian-born, and as one of the early industrial psychologists, was rather well known. The author of several books, Révész was a professor at the University of Amsterdam, and also served as a consultant to the Bijenkorf department stores. Members of a Dutch Jewish family named Isaac were the major stockholders in Bijenkorf. When they were made aware of the Broesslers' plight, the Isaacs agreed to help get Eva and Ruth out of Vienna and to keep Ruth with them until Gustav and Thekla could leave Austria. Arrangements would be made for Eva to stay with the Isaacs' cousins, the Simons family.[26]

The decision to transport the girls to The Netherlands was also based on the recollection that the Dutch had been good to children who had been sent there during World War I. Gustav and Thekla believed that Eva and Ruth would be free and safe there and that the girls would be able to continue their schooling until their parents could come for them, hopefully in no longer than six months. Eva remembers that although, like most adolescents, she was caught up in herself to some degree, she was aware of the danger they were all in. While she did not want to leave home, she understood the necessity of doing so.[27]

As noted earlier, Eva and her family were at this time living with an aunt because they had been evicted from their apartment as part of the German effort to step up the pressure on those Jews who still remained in Austria. It took several weeks to complete the paperwork for emigration through the Zentralstelle and to get passports for Eva and Ruth. Fifteen-year-old Eva, seven-year-old Ruth and their father had to stand in line for hours in order to pick up the passports. But, in the end, Eva and Ruth had the required documents. The passports were issued by the Third Reich, since Austrians were now considered to be German citizens, and were stamped with a "J," identifying the girls as Jews. The girls signed them with their full names: Eva Gertrud Broessler and Ruth Sylvia Broessler.[28]

The girls' journey to the Netherlands began on January 31, 1939.[29] Eva can only imagine how her parents must have felt at that point, sending their daughters away, holding back the tears as they left. Just fifteen, Eva felt that she would now have to become like a mother to her young sister. She remembers that the two of them were well dressed on the day they left Vienna, recalling especially the red hat her sister wore. They had to walk to the train station, as Jews were forbidden to ride the city's streetcars, and the husband of their former housekeeper helped carry their luggage, a violation of the law forbidding association with Jews. It was all moving, sad, and traumatic, but Eva was glad that her sister was with her.[30] The girls were not traveling on a *Kindertransport*, the famous trains by which thousands of Austrian Jewish children escaped to Great Britain, but on a standard international train. They rode as regular passengers during the entire trip. The sisters shared a compartment, along with six other children, whose parents had also decided to send them to safety.[31] Among the children sharing the compartment with them were two boys named Bettelheim, who Eva thinks may have been nephews of Bruno Bettelheim, the famed Austrian-born child psychologist.[32]

In retrospect, thinking back on that time, Eva believes that having Ruth with her is what helped to save her own life. Eva met the age limit for children who were sent from Austria to safe havens abroad, but she believes that the factor which mattered the most in securing her a place on that train was her role as Ruth's guardian for the trip. Had she not been with Ruth, Eva is not sure that she would have been permitted to leave Austria by herself.[33]

The train trip was both frightening and exciting for the two girls. They were allowed to bring very little money with them, and knew the border crossing into The Netherlands could be difficult. At the same time, the girls found being on an international train with a dining car thrilling; Eva recalls eating in the dining car and trying turtle soup for the first time. Most of all, Eva felt numb and didn't really have any sense of danger. She attributes this feeling to trying to reject the trauma of leaving her parents and her home and to keep things feeling as normal as possible. Ruth's recollections of the trip are those of being in somewhat of a daze as they left Austria, but she too had no obvious sense of panic and was glad to be with Eva. The train passed through Cologne, Germany late at night, and made a stop there. Here the girls made a daring and risky decision. Knowing that Cologne was a magnificent city with a famous gothic cathedral, Eva and Ruth got off the train for a bit and looked around. For a short while, the sisters could repress their anxieties and pretend that everything was normal; that they were two young tourists enjoying the sights of the city. They passed by the cathedral and they took note of the differences between Cologne and Vienna. For example, the streetcars there were a different color, not red as they were in Vienna. This was clear and definite proof that they were no longer in Austria and that they had embarked on a journey that would affect them for the rest of their lives.[34] Looking back on their Cologne adventure, Eva would say that the significance of their leaving the train was in the rebelliousness of the act. Forced to leave their home, the clandestine tour of Cologne, brief as it was, served as a protest to the situation Eva and Ruth found themselves in.[35]

Upon arriving in The Netherlands, the children passed successfully through the border station and customs office. Their luggage was searched, but nothing was taken from them. Eva had some gold bracelets with her, and she was happily surprised to see that they had not been confiscated. Now that they were in The Netherlands, there was a sense of excitement in the air. Everything was new; the currency, the language—but there was an unwelcome surprise waiting for the girls. Eva and Ruth had expected to be delivered to the Isaac and Simons families, but a new Dutch regulation required that the girls and the other children, as well as adult Jews who had entered Holland, be "quarantined." The girls were placed in the Heijplaat internment camp near Rotterdam, along with the other children who had traveled with them. Eva believes that the law was enacted as a response to Dutch complaints about illegal border crossings into The Netherlands. These camps would give the Dutch the opportunity to sort out legal immigrants from those who had entered the country illegally.[36]

The camp Eva and Ruth were assigned to had only Jewish refugees. Ten to fifteen people shared a room; at first Ruth and Eva were placed together, but after a week or so, the girls were separated. Eva was issued a pillow when they arrived at the camp, but for some reason, Ruth did not receive one. Eva gave hers to Ruth.[37] To this day, Ruth feels ashamed that she accepted it. The girls spent about eight weeks in the camp. Eva passed the time by writing letters, cleaning, and performing other assigned duties. The experience was not completely unpleasant for her as she met others her own age and made friends.[38]

Ruth found the experience to be more traumatic. After she and Eva were separated, Ruth was placed in a one-story building with other Jewish children around her age, but most were the children of Orthodox Jews and they were more religious than she. It was Ruth's first experience in a strongly religious Jewish environment, and it was an alien and frightening one. For Ruth the religious services and the songs celebrating the Sabbath were strange, especially as they were conducted in Hebrew. Ruth wanted nothing to do with the others and desperately wished to leave the camp. Eva could go and see Ruth whenever she desired, but that was not enough to offset the situation. What made the experience bearable was that they had occasional visitors: the mothers of the Simons and Isaac families and Magda Révész each came to see the girls. On two occasions they were able to take Eva and Ruth to visit Amsterdam.[39]

Finally, on March 27, 1939, about two months after their internment, the girls were released from the camp and were permitted to go and live with their benefactors in The Hague. Eva went to the home of Marinus and Caroline Simons, who had three daughters of their own: Jobje (Sophie Marianne), Hannie (Hannie Estella), and Tin (Judith). Eva would live with the Simons family until September of 1940, and the three girls struck up a friendship that has lasted down to the present. (Marinus and Caroline perished at Bergen-Belsen in 1945.[40] Jobje's sisters survived transport to concentration camps, including Auschwitz, while Jobje, having escaped from a Dutch concentration camp, lived underground with Eva for most of the occupation.)[41]

Ruth, meanwhile, moved in with the Isaac family, Frits (Siegfried) and Elly, who had two children, Arthur and Jet, who were about her age. As the major stockholders in the Bijenkorf department stores in The Netherlands, the Isaacs were wealthy and Ruth found herself in an educated and intellectual environment. Ruth was sent to a Montessori school, an expensive proposition, but one the Isaacs could afford. Ruth quickly learned Dutch. Both girls now were living in much more secure and comfortable circumstances than those they had left in their homeland, but, even so, they were both homesick until they adjusted to the new language and customs. Although they were living in different homes, the girls saw each other frequently and often talked by telephone.[42]

Like her sister, Eva learned Dutch quickly, but she did not attend a regular school in The Hague. Instead, she opted to learn a trade, thinking that would be of greater use to her when she arrived in America. So Eva took courses in sewing and hat making. She attended a trade school for millinery, but did not take any other courses there. Eva found it to be a boring experience; the courses were taught by old-fashioned elderly women and the course seemed more like an apprenticeship. The other girls were from a different economic and perhaps intellectual background, and Eva had little contact with them. She spent her free time reading books rather than socializing with the others.[43]

What may also have made the first months in The Netherlands easier for Eva and Ruth was their certain belief that the separation from their parents would last only a few months. Gustav and Thekla expected that they would soon be able to join their daughters, and then they would wait together for their visas to the United States to come through. That was expected to take no more than a year, hopefully less. But circumstances conspired against an early reunion for the Broesslers. Before Gustav and Thekla could make their way to The Netherlands, the Dutch closed their borders to further immigration. Although they were devastated by the news of the border closing, their fortunes took a turn for the better when they received interim entry permits to Great Britain, thanks to the efforts of Lord (Sir David) and Lady Olga Milne-Watson.

The assistance of Lord and Lady Milne-Watson was the result of a rather fortunate circumstance. The Broesslers' former housekeeper and nanny, Mitzi (in England called Maria) Ponlechner, had left Austria earlier for England and had become a cook for the Milne-Watsons. After learning of the Broesslers' situation back home, Maria approached her employers and asked them if they could possibly help Gustav and Thekla escape from Austria. Lady Olga, who was active in working for charitable foundations, consulted with Lady Rothschild about whether or not she and Sir David should assist the Broesslers. She asked Lady Rothschild for advice since Lord Rothschild was the chairman of a group called the Emigration Committee. This organization had been established in 1936 to help German Jews leave Germany. Her husband's work with this committee more than likely led Lady Rothschild to encourage the Milne-Watsons to assist the Broesslers. Mitzi's request was agreed to and entry permits for Eva and Ruth's parents were obtained and forwarded to them.[44]

Gustav and Thekla left Austria as quickly as they could. Their journey to England went through The Hague, and their travel papers permitted them to visit with Eva and Ruth. Their time together would be short as Gustav and Thekla were only allowed to stay for a week. Both girls were overjoyed to see their parents once again. Gustav and Thekla stayed at the Simons' home, but because both the Isaac and Simons families had left for a vacation in Switzerland, leaving Eva and Ruth in the care of other relatives, the girls' parents never had the chance to meet their daughters' Dutch patrons. Both girls were glad to see their parents safely away from Nazi-controlled Austria, but they were upset by the knowledge that they would soon be separated again. The girls sustained themselves with the hope that they would join their parents in England before much longer and, once there, they would all be able to leave for the United States.[45] The Broesslers were to be bitterly disappointed when events took their lives in a new direction.

World War II in Europe began on September 1, 1939. Eva was at the beach on that day, along with the Simons family, and they learned about the outbreak of hostilities from the extra-edition newspapers. Eva understood that the situation had just become potentially more dangerous, but she, like every other Jewish refugee in The Netherlands, had no idea where else they could go. Germany had not declared war on the Dutch, and everyone hoped that the country would remain neutral in this conflict as it had in World War I.[46]

Gustav and Thekla had arrived safely in England the month before and were taken to the Milne-Watson's estate near the Dorset coast. The estate, over 1,200 acres, was called Ashley Chase, and had been purchased by Sir

David some years earlier. The estate included a farm and the remains of a thirteenth-century Cistercian monastery, but the majority of the land remained wooded and was an ideal setting for the hunting and shooting parties Sir David hosted.[47] There the Broesslers could wait for their U.S. immigration quota number to come up, and then could retrieve Eva and Ruth so that the four of them could sail to America together.[48] The German invasion of Poland in September shattered that dream and, although the Broesslers could not have known it at the time, destined them all to a separation that would last until well after the war's end.

There was a gardener's house on the estate, and it was in this modest residence that Gustav and Thekla lived while they stayed with the Milne-Watsons. Located some distance from the manor house, the bungalow was without electricity and the nearest village was several miles from the estate. Isolated and frequently alone, the Broesslers endured a forlorn existence for the next year.[49] Gustav and Thekla worried about the safety of their daughters, and even though they corresponded regularly the fears were in no way lessened. They pleaded with their benefactors to use whatever influence they could bring to bear to help bring Eva and Ruth out of The Netherlands. Regretfully, the Milne-Watsons found themselves unable to overcome the bureaucratic hurdles that would have allowed them to help the Broesslers reunite in England.[50] The fact that they had assisted Gustav and Thekla was remarkable in of itself, as the general attitude of the British aristocracy toward Germany, at least up to the invasion of Poland, tended to be favorable.

When the Milne-Watsons did spend time at Ashley Chase, they expected the Broesslers to dine with them. Since neither Gustav nor Thekla spoke much English, their time with the Milne-Watsons was awkward, to say the least, as well as lonely. Dinners with their benefactors were formal affairs with proper etiquette the order of the day. The Broesslers were seated at a long wooden table with Thekla by Sir David at one end, and Gustav next to Lady Olga at the other end. Servants were ever present, and both the Milne-Watsons and Broesslers must have felt ill at ease.

Life for the divided family settled into a routine over the next several months. Once Poland was overrun and divided between Germany and Soviet Union, a period of uneasy calm set in over Western Europe. Although the Soviets invaded Finland, Germany made no further aggressive moves, and eventually people began talking of a "Phony War," or *Sitzkrieg*. Eva and Ruth settled into their lives in Holland, just as their anxious parents did in Great Britain. The girls' fluency in Dutch improved rapidly; Ruth continued to attend school and Eva progressed in her efforts to master sewing and millinery. The girls visited each other as often as they could, and they spoke on the phone frequently. In England, Gustav and Thekla endured their separation from their daughters and waited for the day when they would all be together again.

But in the spring of 1940, the German war machine came to life once again, dashing the hopes of Gustav and Thekla. Denmark and Norway were quickly overrun, and the *Wehrmacht* turned toward the Low Countries. On May 10, 1940, Hitler's forces crossed the border into The Netherlands. The country fell in five days. With the entry of the German forces into The Netherlands, the two girls found themselves trapped there. The war had indeed come to them.[51]

NOTES

1. Weissman, *Shoah*.
2. Weissman, *Life*.
3. Hilsenrad, 253, 265.
4. Hilsenrad, 205.
5. Weissman, *Shoah*.
6. Ibid; Newmark, *Shoah*; Weissman, *Life*. Innitzer had church bells rung when the Germans marched into Austria, and Nazi flags were hung from Catholic churches by his order. Innitzer was eventually censured by the Vatican for his actions.
7. The Gestapo *(Geheime Staatspolizei)* was the official secret police of Nazi Germany. Empowered to investigate cases of treason and espionage, the Gestapo also supervised concentration camps and was not subject to judicial oversight. Department IV, section B5 dealt specifically with the Jewish population.
8. The SA *(Sturmabteilung)* was the Nazi Party's paramilitary organization. The SA carried out acts of violence against opposing political parties in Germany in the 1920s and helped Hitler rise to power. After Hitler came to power, the SA often participated in riots against Jews but by the time of the Anschluss it had lost much of its influence.
9. Hilsenrad, 277–279; Friedländer, 242.
10. Built in March 1933, Dachau was the first concentration camp constructed by the Nazi regime. Located in Germany about ten miles from Munich, Dachau served as a model for the construction of later concentration camps.
11. Weissman, *Shoah*; Ruth Broessler, *My Life* (unpublished memoir).
12. Weissman, *Shoah*.
13. HC, 122; "Austria," Shoah Resource Center, www.yadvashem.org.
14. Broessler, *My Life*.
15. Ibid; Weissman, *Life*.
16. "Austria," Shoah Resource Center, www.yadvashem.org; Friedländler, 239.
17. Weissman, *Life*.
18. Newmark, *Shoah*; Friedländer, 243.
19. Weissman, *Shoah*.
20. Hilsenrad, 279; "Vienna," Shoah Resource Center, www.yadvashem.org.

21. Friedländer, 244–245.
22. Broessler, *My Life*; Newmark, *Shoah*; Weissman, *Shoah*.
23. Newmark, *Memoir*, 9–10.
24. Newmark, *Shoah*; Broessler, *My Life*; Weissman, *Life*.
25. Robert L. Beir and Brian Josepher, *Roosevelt and the Holocaust: A Rooseveltian Examines the Poliices and Remembers the Times* (Fort Lee, NJ: Barricade Books, 2006), 155–158.
26. Weissman, *Life*.
27. Weissman, *Life*.
28. Ibid; Broessler, *My Life*.
29. Weissman to Moore, August 25, 2005.
30. Broessler, *My Life*; Weissman, *Life*.
31. Broessler, *My Life*; Weissman, *Life*.
32. Weissman, *Shoah*. Bettelheim had been interned at Dachau in 1938 and was still there when Eva and Ruth left Vienna. He was released later in 1939 and left Austria for Australia later that year. He emigrated from Australia to the United States in 1943.
33. Weissman to Moore, August 25, 2005.
34. Weissman, *Life;* Weissman to Moore, August 25, 2005.
35. Ibid.
36. Weissman, *Life*; Weissman, *Shoah*; Weissman to Moore, August 25, 2005.
37. Weissman, *Shoah*; Weissman, *Life*.
38. Ibid.
39. Ibid.
40. Originally built to be a camp for prisoners of war, Bergen-Belsen was converted into a concentration camp in 1942; more than 50,000 people perished there.
41. Eva G. Weissman, "Personal Notes in Honor of the Dutch Family Simons," November 9, 2001 (hereafter *Personal Notes*); Weissman, *Shoah*; Weissman to Moore, August 25, 2005.
42. Weissman, *Shoah,* Weissman, *Life*; Broessler, *My Life*.
43. Ibid; Weissman, *Shoah*.
44. Newmark, *Memoir*, 12, note 23; Weissman, *Life*.
45. Weissman, *Life*.
46. Weissman, *Life*.
47. Newmark, *Memoir*, 49.
48. Broessler, *My Life*; Weissman, *Shoah*.
49. Newmark, *Memoir*, 49.
50. Ibid.
51. Ibid.

Chapter Three

Trapped in The Netherlands

German troops crossed the Dutch border at 3 a.m. on the morning of May 10, 1940. By May 15, The Netherlands surrendered and the Nazi occupation of that country got underway. The occupation went through four stages.

The first stage lasted from May of 1940 until the spring of 1941. In this period the occupation, under the direction of High Commissioner Arthur Seyss-Inquart, created a supervisory commission.[1] Food was gradually rationed, workers were recruited for labor in Germany and the Dutch socialist parties were subordinated under a Dutch National Socialist commissioner. Nazi propaganda, however, led to friction with the Dutch population after a few months. Greater tension would occur over the anti-Jewish policies of the Dutch National Socialist Movement (NSB) and those of the Germans as well. The result, in February 1941, was a general strike in Amsterdam. It was during this period that the first registrations of those persons of Jewish ancestry began to take place.

The next stage of the occupation got underway in the spring of 1941 and would last for close to two years as the conflict between the Dutch population and the Germans increased in intensity. The escalation of the clash between the Dutch and their occupiers can be traced to a number of factors. For one thing, German efforts to conciliate the Dutch in the first year of the occupation had clearly failed. Secondly, the German invasion of the Soviet Union had raised the possibility that the Nazis could be defeated. Finally, the Germans radicalized their policies in the occupied lands and by doing so they increased the tension between themselves and the Dutch. Among the more extreme measures adopted by the Germans were stricter rationing, compulsory registration for all unemployed workers (1942), and the removal of certain select groups of specialists to work in Germany. Tensions with the population were enhanced by the German effort to Nazify Dutch life through steps such as the dissolution of political parties. In the summer of 1941, the process of segregating and concentrating Dutch Jews in Amsterdam got underway; deportations would begin a year afterward.

In the third phase, lasting approximately from the spring of 1943 to September 1944, the conflict between the Dutch population and the Germans continued to intensify, largely due to news of German defeats both in the Mediterranean and at Stalingrad. All efforts to indoctrinate the Dutch population were abandoned and harsher policies were enacted. The deportation of Jews from the country had been nearly completed by this time, with the exception of those like Eva who were still in hiding or those small groups of Jews who remained in camps in The Netherlands, such as Westerbork or Vught.

The fourth stage of the occupation covered the last months of the war, from September 1944 to the German surrender on May 8, 1945. With the approach of the Allied armies, the Germans conducted themselves as if they were holding enemy territory with a hostile population within. Dutch men of military age were drafted into German work gangs, or arrested in order to keep them from assisting the Allies. The Netherlands was stripped of as much of its industrial capacity as possible. Earlier curfew hours were established in the summer of 1944, food rations were cut drastically and rationing of coal-based utilities (electricity and gas) became even stricter. Telephone and telegraph communications were cut and electric train schedules were sharply reduced. Meanwhile, Dutch resistance increased. Acts of sabotage grew in number and more effort was given to intelligence activities. There was also a railroad strike, more activity by the underground press and a greater amount of assistance given to people in hiding. It seems clear that the rise in resistance efforts was directly correlated to the progress of the Allies.[2]

For Gustav and Thekla, the news of the invasion and the subsequent conquest of The Netherlands was a terrible blow. All communications between the girls and their parents were cut off, and there was now no way for the family to be reunited. Adding to the distress of Gustav and Thekla was that in England they were now classified as enemy aliens. The British rounded up Austrians, Czechs, and Germans after France fell. The British gave little regard to whether these persons were sympathetic to the Nazis or were refugees who had fled the Germans after they had taken over their homelands. Males designated as enemy aliens were placed in internment camps. Those who were not apprehended were required to move away from the coast because of growing concerns about a German invasion. Gustav was taken from Ashley Chase and interned on the Isle of Man and Thekla was forced to move to London. There she was able to stay with a Viennese-born cousin named Elsa Kronberger.[3]

Launched on a Friday, the German attack began early in the morning of May 10, 1940, and caught the Dutch by surprise. The population of Amsterdam was awakened at four in the morning by the sound of aircraft roaring overhead and anti-aircraft guns shooting at them. While such sounds had been heard since the war's beginning in 1939, this time they were more intense and threatening. Those who looked out their windows saw dozens of German planes flying over the city. Radio announcements confirmed what the appearance of the aircraft meant, as paratrooper landings were reported throughout the country. Resistance to the invasion quickly collapsed and when word came that the Dutch Government had fled to England, the people of The Netherlands knew the war was over for them.[4]

There was widespread fear and dejection among the Dutch at the beginning of the occupation, and these feelings were not just restricted to the Jews. Many tried to escape or committed suicide, while numerous others tried to flee by boat. Many Jews made their way to the harbor at Ijmuiden, apparently in response to a rumor that the Dutch government had provided a special ship to transport Dutch Jews to England. Some Jews were able to board a ship called the *Bodegraven*, which did sail out around 8 p.m. on May 10 and several hundred Jews escaped The Netherlands successfully. But confusion among various Dutch government officials seems to have kept most people from boarding any vessels and many were turned back from the port. Those who made their way to the port had to endure overcrowded roads and were in danger of being attacked by German warplanes, often taking shelter in roadside ditches as German planes flew overhead.[5]

As the Germans entered the country, the Simons family, with whom Eva was staying, were among those who decided to flee to England. They packed their daughters into their car and left The Hague, hoping to board a ship or hire a boat at the nearby port of Scheveningen. Eva refused to go with the Simons, however, insisting that she had to remain behind because she had to take care of Ruth. Unable to board a ship or find a boat to hire, the Simons family had no choice but to return home.[6] For the next several days, rumors swirled through The Netherlands as the Germans took control of the country. The rumors fueled fears that a pogrom would soon occur, which caused a panic and resulted in a number of suicides among Jews, with thirty reported in The Hague alone. As many as 200 Jews may have taken their own lives, most of them German refugees who could no longer stand to live under Nazi rule again. In some cases, entire families chose death over life under Nazi rule, and long rows of newly dug graves appeared in the Jewish cemetery within a week of the German invasion. When a new rumor, which proved to be false, suggested that Jews could still apply for exit visas, many allegedly arrived at government offices with bandaged throats and wrists. After a brief period, however, life returned to some semblance of normality.[7]

For Eva and Ruth's parents the knowledge that their daughters were once again under the Nazi yoke was undoubtedly made doubly hard to bear when word came in August that their American visas had finally been issued in London. Gustav was released from internment and was reunited with Thekla. The reunion occurred on a passenger ship bound for the United States, one of the last to leave for America before German U-boats made the Atlantic passage too dangerous. Gustav was escorted to the ship by a pair of plainclothes policemen, but as Eva recalls the story, a friend of her parents who witnessed Gustav's arrival said that he carried himself so well that it appeared as if it was he who was escorting the pair of policemen.[8] One can only imagine the heartbreak the two of them felt as they watched the British coast disappear over the horizon, knowing that their daughters remained trapped in the Nazi-occupied Netherlands and that they might not see them ever again. The Broesslers arrived safely in the United States, landing in New York City with the equivalent of ten dollars in their pockets. As they thought about what they would do next, Gustav and Thekla stayed with Thekla's brother, Max Lampl, his wife, Pauline, and their twelve-year-old son, as well as with Thekla's other brother, Felix, and his wife, Hilda. Work, for one thing, would not be easy to come by. Despite the efforts of the Roosevelt Administration's New Deal policies, the prospects for employment for a pair of new immigrant arrivals in New York City were poor. Through a Jewish resettlement agency Gustav and Thekla were able to arrange to go to Indianapolis by bus, hoping that the prospects for employment might be better there. Taking nothing but one suitcase in which to carry their possessions, the couple journeyed to Indianapolis where they learned that conditions were no better. The resettlement agency, however, told them that there were jobs in northern Indiana, particularly in Michigan City. The agency provided Gustav and Thekla with bus fare to that city, and with their hopes revived, they headed north. Once in Michigan City, they found that the job market was indeed more promising. Both found employment with a Jewish family-owned firm called Society Lingerie. Without previous experience, Gustav began working as a cutter in the factory, while Thekla was hired as a sewing machine operator. Thekla would eventually work her way up to a supervisory position on the factory floor, and then to manager of the company's outlet shop. For the Broesslers, the situation was something of a role reversal compared to their lives in Europe, as they were the only non-management Jews employed by the company.[9]

Back in The Netherlands Eva and Ruth found themselves returning to the conditions that had caused the family to flee from Austria, while the Simons and Isaac families now experienced the kinds of things that had brought the girls to them originally. Anti-Jewish regulations were enacted continuously throughout the next two years. After the occupation, the rumors that Jews would be persecuted had proved to be false, and some level of relaxation had set in. When the first sets of anti-Jewish regulations were enacted, Dutch Jews complied with them. With the implementation of the Nuremberg Laws in The Netherlands in January 1941, which required all Jews to register with the state, most did so, not realizing that the basic census information they were giving the Nazis would provide the Germans with what they needed to carry out later round-ups and deportations.[10]

Just as the occupation went through several phases, so did the process of persecuting the Jewish population, both native Dutch Jews and Jewish refugees. The initial stage was implemented soon after the occupation and would continue into the summer of 1941. It began with the elimination of all Jews from public life and positions of influence. Radios were confiscated and Jews were segregated from Gentiles by exclusion from recreational facilities, hotels and restaurants. Registration of Jewish businesses had begun several months earlier, and that process was culminated with the order for their compulsory sale in March 1941. In May of that year the registration and sale of agrarian property owned by Jews commenced. To this point no real physical persecution of Jews took place, belying earlier rumors that Jews would be attacked by the Germans or that pogroms would take place shortly after the conquest of the country was completed.[11]

There was, however, in February 1941, an episode of open armed resistance by Dutch Jews. Provoked by the marches and attacks of Nazi storm troopers, some working-class Amsterdam Jews formed what they called "Action Groups," or *Knokploegen*, in response. Some fighting broke out between these Action Groups and the NSB, and a number of NSB members were wounded and one was killed. The Nazis reacted swiftly and ruthlessly. Some 400 young Jews were arrested and sent to Mauthausen, an extermination camp located in Austria. In June, another 230 Jewish youths were arrested and deported to Mauthausen where they were worked to death (only one of them somehow survived the war) in reprisal for the planting of a time bomb in Amsterdam. Following the events of February, the Germans established a Jewish Council (*Joodsche Raad*) in Amsterdam to assist in the administration of Jewish affairs. The Council was modeled on the centuries-old Prague *Judenrat*, and was formed as part of a European-wide German effort to identify and select Jewish leaders who could then be used to administer German affairs.[12]

Prior to the creation of the Jewish Council, a Jewish Coordinating Committee (*Joodsche Coördinatie Commissie*) had been organized in December 1940. The goal of this group was to provide help to Dutch Jews while avoiding collaboration with the Germans. The chairman of the committee was Lodewijk Visser, who had been named to the Dutch Supreme Court in 1939, only to be removed shortly after the German occupation began. Frits Isaac and his brother-in-law, Henri Edersheim, were members of this organization, with Edersheim serving as Secretary of the Coordinating Committee. This organization differed ideologically from the German-organized Jewish Council. Visser was of the view that the Dutch administration was constitutionally obligated to aid the Dutch people, including the Jewish population, and the Coordinating Committee refused to cooperate with the occupation.

The Jewish Council, led by a diamond merchant and member of the Liberal Party named Abraham Asscher, and David Cohen, professor of Ancient History at the Municipal University of Amsterdam, argued that since The Netherlands was now under German rule, the Dutch Jews had no choice but to cooperate with the authorities. Many, Frits and Elly Issac among them, felt that the Council was merely an arm of the German occupation, created to carry out their plans for the Jewish population. Both Asscher and Cohen were given the responsibility of making all decisions that might be required; this action isolated them from the other members of the Council and may have made them more susceptible to German pressure. Members of the Council were criticized for joining and were accused of doing so in order to protect themselves and their relatives. Council members, on the other hand, felt they were genuinely doing a service and that they could prevent worse from happening.[13]

The next level of persecutions began in June 1941, coinciding with the German invasion of the Soviet Union, and would continue until July 1942. The Jews were now isolated even more and preparations began for deportations of Jews to Eastern Europe. A branch of the main security office of the SS, the Central Agency for Jewish Emigration (*Zentralstelle für Jüdische Auswanderung*) was established in Amsterdam to supervise the deportations. Further isolation was accomplished by excluding Jewish students from non-Jewish educational institutions and Jews were required to resign from all non-Jewish organizations to which they belonged. In April 1942, Jews were made to wear the yellow Star of David in public. They were also required to deposit their funds in special blocked accounts in certain designated banks that were managed by German officials. They were then allowed to withdraw only small monthly allowances from these accounts. Jews also had to register any real estate holdings under German supervision and were expected to arrange for their disposal at some time in the future. Employers could now fire Jews at will and Jews were banned from certain professions. Unemployed, and eventually, even employed Jews were sent to labor camps inside The Netherlands.

The persecution of Jews in The Netherlands entered a new stage in June 1942. This began with the announcement on June 26, 1942 by the Zentralstelle to the Jewish Council that Jews were going to be conscripted for labor in Germany and that the initial group would leave in the middle of July. To prepare for this, security forces stepped up the process of isolating the Jewish population even more. Bicycles were confiscated, Jews could no longer use public transportation, and a curfew was enforced against them. Furthermore, Jews could only shop during special hours and they could no longer make telephone calls.

The last stage of the persecution began in October 1943. With most of the Jewish population in The Netherlands now deported, attention turned to those remaining in the transit camps or who were on exempted lists. Efforts to identify and apprehend Jews in hiding increased. Once the main groups of Jews had been transported from the transit camps, small maintenance groups were left behind. Jewish affairs that had been under the administration of the Jewish Council were now placed under the control of Jews who had exemptions because they were in mixed marriages.[14]

These events were all too familiar to Eva and Ruth. As the regulations increased the limitations upon them, they again found themselves forbidden to use any form of public transportation, nor could they go to any public place. Ruth could no longer attend the private Montessori school she had been going to; now she had to attend a separate school for Jewish children. As they had done everywhere else, the Nazis confiscated Jewish belongings: houses, money, insurance, gold, silver, jewelry, cars, radios, bicycles, and anything else they could think of. There was an early evening curfew and Jews and Gentiles were no longer allowed to visit each other.[15] Their Dutch identification cards (carried by all persons fifteen years of age or older) were now stamped with a "J." The critical feature of German police control over the Dutch population, the cards also had the owner's signature, fingerprints and photograph on them. Failure to carry the card at all times when out in public carried grave consequences. By stamping their identification cards with the "J," the Germans could immediately differentiate the Jewish population from the Gentiles.[16] Even so, conditions in The Netherlands were a bit different than they had been in Austria when Eva and Ruth had left. There had been very few physical attacks on Jews, for one thing, and most Dutch did not support the Nazis.

The regulation requiring Jews to wear a yellow Star of David on their clothes was meant to make them even more easily identifiable. Eva recalls having to stitch the emblem on her clothing.[17] Living under such conditions was very difficult, yet Eva would explain years later that you knew you had to "take it" and that the Nazis were doing worse things elsewhere. There was a definite sense of danger, even hopelessness. Eva feared that she would never get out of The Netherlands, although her parents had done everything they could to reunite the family.[18] Ruth thought that wearing the yellow star was just another regulation to be endured, but she found that wearing the emblem made her angry. That anger was rarely expressed, however, because no one knew for certain who they could trust or who might turn them in for expressing anti-Nazi feelings. The Isaacs learned that lesson the hard way, when their cook turned the family in to the Gestapo for hoarding food. Fortunately, the Gestapo only confiscated the food and did not arrest anyone.[19]

In the late summer of 1940, the Germans decreed that foreigners could no longer live on the Dutch coastline. This meant that Eva could not stay with the Simons family in The Hague, although because of her age, Ruth was able to remain with the Isaacs. Marinus Simons' mother and a sister lived in Utrecht and they agreed to take Eva in. Marianne Simons van Raalte (Oma Simons) was the widow of a law professor at the University of Utrecht; her unmarried daughter, Dr. Estella Simons, whom Eva would come to call "Tante Stel," was an attorney. Although they were old-fashioned and protective, the women were loving and inspirational to Eva. Eva missed the Simons' household in The Hague where there were three girls her own age. The house Marianne and Estella lived in was large enough to require domestic help, but some time after Eva arrived the Gestapo confiscated the property and assigned them to a smaller house. The domestic staff could not go with them because they were not Jewish. Eva lived with Marianne and Estella for two years, from September 1940 to August 1942.[20]

Once again, Eva settled into the routine of life as a foreign Jewish girl in a Nazi-occupied country. One pleasurable aspect of life was that she had discovered that she could communicate with her parents through the Sugars who were refugees in Venezuela, or through family friends in Portugal, who would forward letters from Eva to her parents. She could also write to relatives in Vienna.[21] Although Eva's letters to her parents arrived infrequently, they had to be a source of great comfort for Gustav and Thekla. The Germans, however, monitored the mails and foreign mail was routinely censored.[22]

The lives of Eva and Ruth were altered dramatically in the summer of 1942. Beginning on July 14, the Nazis began deporting the Jews in The Netherlands to death camps in Poland. This event affected the girls in different ways. Ruth's foster family decided to attempt an escape to Switzerland in an effort to save their lives. Before Ruth and the Isaacs would make their daring attempt, however, circumstances forced Eva to change her identity and become a "hidden person" in Amsterdam. She would remain so until the end of the war.

The announcement in late June 1942 that Dutch Jews would have to go to Germany to work under police supervision aroused intense feelings of dismay within the Jewish community, and doubts and fears about their eventual destiny began to surface. For one thing, the issue of physical survival had to be confronted, and many naturally made efforts to remain in The Netherlands rather than be forced to leave for an unknown destination and fate. On the day the first group of Jews selected for transport were required to report to the Zentralstelle, only a few showed up. The Nazi response was to carry out a series of mass raids in which some 750 Jews were arrested. These people were held hostage in order to coerce those who had been ordered to report for deportation to do so. The tactic worked to some extent through the end of July as about 6,000 Jews were transported to Westerbork and from there to the death camps.[23]

Yet, in August, the numbers dropped off. The German authority had an extra edition of the *Joodsche Weekblad (Jewish Weekly)* published in order to announce that those who were ordered to report for deportation and failed to do so would be arrested and sent to Mauthausen; in effect, this was a blatant death threat. The Germans followed up the announcement with a pair of raids in Amsterdam in which thousands of Jews were taken into custody. Most of these were released later, although some escaped from the staging area as they were being organized for transport to either Westerbork or Vught. Nonetheless, turnout remained poor. To this point the Germans had simply mailed out a summons to those families that had been chosen for transportation; now they began to change their methods. Those assigned for deportation began to be rounded up during nighttime raids, although the mail system remained in effect. Night raids became a regular feature of life in September with 300 to 500 Jews being arrested each time. It was also in September 1942 that an exemption system was formalized through the provision of exemption stamps (*Sperrstempel*). These stamps became highly prized possessions among Dutch Jews.[24] Interestingly, once the deportations began, it is estimated that just some 20,000 Jews in The Netherlands attempted to go underground (approximately less than 1 in 6 of those who were to be deported). Of these, about 8,000, half of whom were children, survived.[25]

It was an unfortunate incident that led to Eva's identity change and sent her into hiding. One of her friends was the daughter of a Dutch Christian pastor named Oberman. Eva knew that her friend and her family were not Jewish, but she was unaware of the fact that the father was active in the Dutch Resistance. At some point, the Gestapo learned of Oberman's connection with the Resistance, and the pastor was arrested, along with several others, in August 1942. The Nazis confiscated the Oberman family's papers, including the daughter's address book. It was in the address book that the Gestapo discovered Eva's name.[26]

A pair of Gestapo agents came for Eva at her home in Utrecht late at night Tuesday, August 18th. She was arrested and taken to the police station, and on the next day she and others were transferred by police car to a jail in Amsterdam. Recalling the ride later, Eva remembered it as taking place on a vividly beautiful summer's day. Despite the splendor of that August day, Eva knew she was in serious danger. The Germans were aware that she was Jewish, and Eva could only speculate as to what fate awaited her in Amsterdam.[27]

Once in Amsterdam, she was placed in a cell with two other Jewish girls. Eva felt stifled by her confinement, and would later say that her time in jail helped her to realize just how important fresh air is. The austere jail cell contained a bunk bed, a primitive toilet, and a little window through which food was passed. Eva remembers sleeping on the floor, but cannot recall if she had a mattress to lie on or not. Eva and the other girls were permitted brief exercise, which consisted of being taken from the cell to walk around a bit, once a day, under the watchful eyes of the guards. Eva felt "lousy" as she later put it, and, quite naturally, she was afraid. But, as she would state later, "You just didn't sit there and say you were afraid." The nights seemed endless. Eva recalls asking one of her cellmates on the first night of her confinement, "Do the nights always take so long here?"[28]

Although the Gestapo knew Eva was Jewish, it appears at that point that they were only interested in her because they suspected Oberman had involved her in the Resistance. Eva languished in the cell until the weekend. Finally, on Saturday afternoon, August 22nd, the Gestapo officer who had arrested Eva in Utrecht questioned her. The interrogation was a lengthy one, as the German asked Eva dozens of questions about her relationship to the Obermans, and whether or not she knew anything about Pastor Oberman's involvement with the Resistance. Beyond her friendship with the pastor's daughter, Eva knew little about the Oberman family and had no knowledge of the father's association with the Resistance. She insisted that she knew nothing about this, and that her only "crime" was that of being Jewish. Eventually, Eva managed to convince the Gestapo officer of her innocence, or he simply decided to let her go for the time being with the intention of keeping her under observation. Looking back on that day, Eva would comment that "You know only when you are [17 or] 18 would you have the [courage] to say such a thing."[29]

Eva was to be set free, but the officer informed her that since it was the weekend, she would have to remain in Amsterdam. He explained that she would need a permit to board a train back to Utrecht, and the office through which the required documents could be obtained was closed until Monday morning. The officer told Eva that she might have to stay in jail until then. Eva replied that she had friends in Amsterdam with whom she could stay, and the official, surprisingly, agreed to let her go. He reminded her, however, that she would have to return on Monday to collect her train permit. Eva's possessions, which naturally had been taken away upon her arrival at the jail, were now returned to her. She was made to examine her purse in order to be certain everything was there, and then she had to sign a release form. Eva demanded to read the document before signing it, another act of courage or, perhaps, teenaged bravado. After reading the paper, she affixed her signature and was escorted from the jail.[30] Eva then proceeded on foot to a place where she could find help.

Back in Utrecht, Estella Simons had put the word out about Eva's arrest. Among her connections in Amsterdam was a relative of the Simons and Isaac families, Karel Edersheim. It was to Edersheim that Eva now turned. Upon leaving the Gestapo's headquarters, Eva went to see her "Uncle Karel," whose residence was about a half hour's walk from where Eva had been incarcerated. Edersheim, despite having connections to the Jewish Council in Amsterdam, was unaware of Eva's arrest and was unaware that Eva was in Amsterdam until she appeared on his doorstep. She was immediately welcomed, and Eva spent the rest of the weekend with him, his wife and young daughter. Eva told them the story of her arrest and interrogation, and Edersheim was able to get word to the Simons family in Utrecht and in The Hague that Eva was free and safe for the time being.[31]

Now the question was what to do next. On August 24th, the Monday that Eva was to report to Gestapo headquarters to pick up her travel permit, she, Edersheim, Magda Révész, and Estella's first cousin Eka (Erika Grace Line) Simons met to discuss whether or not Eva should return to Utrecht. After some discussion it was decided that going back to Utrecht might be too dangerous for Eva and that she should go underground. In order to make the Gestapo think she had left for Utrecht, however, it was also decided that Eva should go and pick up her travel permit. She simply wouldn't use it. The Gestapo, though, would believe she had done so and wouldn't be likely to think she was still in Amsterdam. Eva would then remove her yellow star and would stay with Eka, a member of another branch of the Simons family. False identification papers would be obtained and Eva would assume a new identity.[32]

After the meeting, Eva left for Gestapo headquarters, which was located on Euterpestraat, to pick up her travel permit. What she was doing was extremely dangerous. Going to Gestapo headquarters could be perilous under the best of circumstances, but on that particular day, the Gestapo was rounding up and arresting Jews for deportation to the death camps, or to hold as hostages until those who had been conscripted for transportation reported as they had been ordered to. Not knowing this, Eva appeared at the school where the Gestapo had set up its headquarters and collected her papers. After she had received her documents, she became confused because the exits were all blocked and she could not find her way out. After wandering around for several minutes, Eva made her way down to the basement. There she discovered an unsecured exit and was able to leave the building.

As soon as she was out of the building, Eva went to the Jewish Council, where she would sign out as all Jews leaving Amsterdam were required to do. It had been decided to have her do this in order to further make it appear that she had indeed left the city. Eva identified herself and presented her travel permit, noting that the Council was aware of her situation. To Eva's surprise, she was greeted with shock and astonishment. At first, the Council members thought Eva was simply advising them that she was on her way to collect the permit, and they told her that she could not go because everyone in the building was being arrested. When Eva told them she had already been to the Gestapo, they did not believe her at first. How could you have been there, they asked. Everyone is being arrested! Eva showed them her travel permit once again and finally convinced them that she had been there and had left without incident.

Eva considers it a miracle that she escaped with her life.[33] Had the German officer decided not to listen when Eva mentioned her relations in Amsterdam, and held her through the weekend, Eva almost certainly would have been detained and sent to the camp at Westerbork, from where she most likely would have been transported to Auschwitz. She was also fortunate that the officer apparently was not responsible for identifying Jews for deportation but for investigating and apprehending members of the Dutch Resistance. Thus, he chose to ignore the fact that Eva was Jewish and permitted her release, trusting that she would return for her documents on Monday. Even more remarkable was her escape from Gestapo headquarters that fateful day. Not only did she collect her papers without incident, she was able to slip away from the clutches of the Gestapo as they were rounding up many of her fellow Jews. Only by the most fortuitous of circumstances did Eva escape deportation from The Netherlands to the death camps in Poland that final week of August 1942.

Now, having signed out of Amsterdam to fool the authorities into thinking she had left for Utrecht, and to prevent the Jewish Council from being accused of hiding her should she be discovered, Eva embarked on the next stage of her life as a refugee. Eka Simons arranged for Eva to move in with her Gentile mother, Johanna Simons. Eka's older brother Siebert and her sister Euphemia (Phemia) also lived with Johanna in Amsterdam. Although she was supposed to stay just a short time with this branch of the Simons family, Eva would remain with them for the rest of the war and for some time afterwards. Eva credits Estella's cousin Eka, whom she remembers as an attractive blonde woman of thirty-one, and her mother with saving her life. Eka was an unmarried laboratory technician who assisted several prominent researchers. In her own memoir, Eka would refer to Eva as the "Austrian girl."[34] (Some time after Eva settled in Amsterdam under her new identity, Marianne and Estella Simons were deported to Theresienstadt, near Prague. Both women survived the concentration camp, and Estella lived to be 100 years old.)[35]

"Mommy Simons," as Johanna was known, was the Christian widow of Philip, a Simons' relative who had died shortly before World War II began. Eva was just one of many Jews to whom Johanna gave refuge during the war, and she would become a personal hero to her. Johanna owned a stationery store, and lived in an upstairs apartment. It was there that she hid a number of Jews, including Eva. She also maintained a cellar hideaway for her charges in the event of Gestapo searches. Johanna clearly was a courageous woman. On more than one occasion she would casually chat with Nazi sympathizers in her store, often while they were standing over the cellar hiding place.[36]

Some weeks later, after joining the Amsterdam Simons family in September, Eva received her new papers. These had been prepared for her by the Dutch Resistance, and they included an identification card with her photograph and fingerprints. Eva now became "Johanna Cornelia Meijer," a Christian girl of nineteen whose occupation was listed as salesclerk in a flower shop. Many people today do not realize how important documents were in those years. They were carried at all times when one was traveling, even on a simple errand in town. These papers were "life or death in those days," Eva recalled, "I was fortunate that I did not have to use them." On one occasion, she was stopped by a policeman for jaywalking. Happily she was not asked to produce her papers. "I do not know if I could have pretended to be Johanna Meijer," Eva admitted.[37]

To this day, Eva knows nothing about the young woman whose identity she assumed. Did the real Johanna Cornelia Meijer "lose" her papers to help the Resistance? Eva does not know, nor has she ever tried to find out. She has considered the possibility that she never truly accepted her new identity, never really thought of herself as someone other than who she truly was. It may have been an act of denial on her part. Eva never tried to find the real Johanna Meijer, perhaps, as she explains, that not doing so reflected a feeling of wanting to forget and since the war was over her false persona was over as well.[38]

NOTES

1. Ironically, Seyss-Inquart, whose family had moved to Austria in 1907, attended the same gymnasium (high school) as Eva's father, Gustav.
2. Werner Warmbrunn, *The Dutch Under German Occupation, 1940–1945* (Stanford: Stanford University Press, 1963), 10–17.
3. Broessler, *My Life*; Weissman, *Life;* Weissman, *Shoah.*
4. Hans Cramer, "A Letter from The Netherlands," Unpublished journal of reminisces of the German occupation of The Netherlands by a German Jewish émigré, translated by Irene Cramer (hereafter Cramer, "Letter").
5. Jacob Presser, *Ashes in the Wind: The Destruction of Dutch Jewry* (Detroit: Wayne State University Press, 1988), 7–8; Warmbrunn, 166, Cramer, "Letter."
6. Newmark, *Shoah*; Interview, Eva Weissman and Gregory Moore, September 22, 2005.
7. Presser, 9–12; Warmbrunn, 166; Cramer, "Letter."
8. Ibid.; Weissman, *Life*; Weissman, *Shoah*.
9. Weissman, *Life*; Newmark, *Shoah*.
10. Warmbrunn, 166.
11. Warmbrunn, 63.
12. Ibid.
13. Warmbrunn, 63–64; Cramer, "Letter"; Newmark, *Memoir*, 20. Ruth recalls a common joke among Dutch Jews that when all of them had been deported, except for Asscher and Cohen, Cohen would then say to Asscher, "You go ahead, Bram, to prevent worse from happening!"
14. Warmbrunn, 63–67.
15. Broessler, *My Life*.
16. Weissman, *Life*; Warmbrunn, 15, 52.
17. Weissman, *Shoah*.
18. Ibid.
19. Newmark, *Shoah*.
20. Weissman, *Shoah*; Weissman, *Life*.
21. Ibid.
22. Warmbrunn, 54.
23. Warmbrunn, 167.
24. Warmbrunn, 167–168. Those granted exemptions included employees and families of the Jewish Council, workers at textile and other critical wartime industries, Jews married to Gentiles, a number of prominent Jews who were given exemptions and held in custody until 1943, when they were sent to Theresienstadt (most survived that camp), those who claimed to have registered as Jews and requested recognition of their Aryan ancestry (these claims were reviewed by the High Commissioner's office), Portuguese Jews who claimed they should be exempted because they were of Mediterranean extraction (most were eventually deported and killed) and Jews who held permits to enter Palestine or were of dual nationality (most of these ended up at

Bergen Belsen where they died from disease, malnutrition, or exhaustion). The Germans also published false exemption lists in order to raise false hopes and to keep Jews from going into hiding. (See Warmbrunn, 66–67.)

25. Warmbrunn, 170.
26. Weissman, *Life,* Weissman, *Shoah.*
27. Correspondence between Eva Weissman and Gregory Moore, June 17, 2005; Weissman, *Shoah,* Weissman, *Life.*
28. Weissman, *Shoah,* Weissman, *Life.*
29. Ibid.
30. Ibid.
31. Ibid.
32. Ibid.
33. Ibid.
34. Weissman, *Personal Notes*; Correspondence between Eva Weissman and Gregory Moore, March 16, 2005.
35. Weissman, *Personal Notes.*
36. Weissman, *Life,* Weissman, *Shoah.*
37. Weissman, *Shoah.*
38. Ibid.

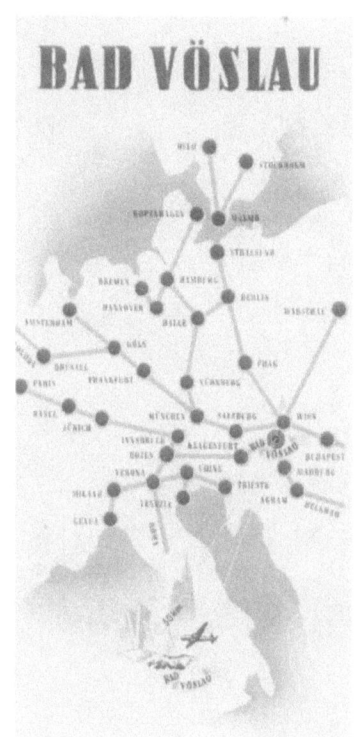

The small town Bad Vöslau, located about eighteen miles from Vienna, Austria, was Eva's universe. As a child, she didn't know that the road to The Netherlands would become her destiny.

The Broessler family home at Bad Vöslau, jokingly referred to by the family as "our castle."

Eva and her father, Gustav Broessler, in 1924.

Eva and her mother, Thekla Broessler, in 1925.

Eva in 1927.

Eva in the garden at Bad Vöslau, 1928.

(Left to Right) Eva with childhood friends Maria (Maria Irmgard) and Lisa (Liselotte Eugenie) Weissenberg at Bad Vöslau, 1928.

(Left to Right) Olga Weissenberg (mother of Eva's childhood friends Maria and Lisa), Eva, Maria Weissenberg and Lisa Weissenberg, in the car of Dr. Eugen Weissenberg (father of Maria and Lisa), September 1928.

The Broessler-Lampl cousins in 1934. (Left to Right) Heinz ("Henry") Lampl, Gertrude ("Trude") Broessler, Peter Broessler, Eva, and Ruth.

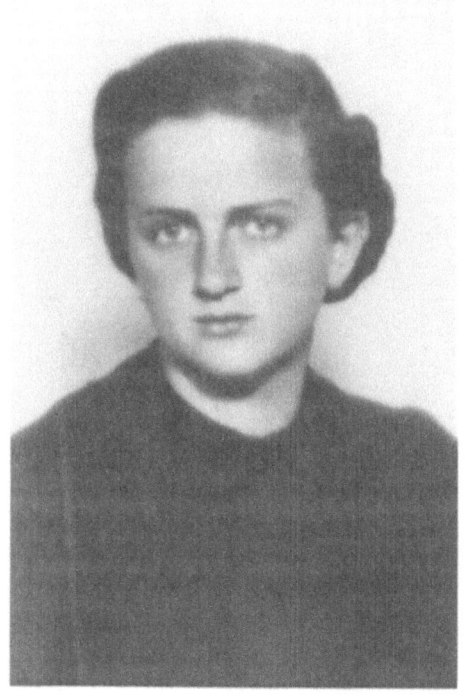

Ada Sugar (Rink), one of Eva's childhood best friends, in 1938.

Gustav and Thekla Broessler, Eva and Ruth's parents, in 1938.

Eva in 1938.

Ruth in 1938.

(Front Row, Left to Right) Judith Simons ("Tin") and Eva (Back Row, Left to Right) Sophie Marianne Simons ("Jobje"), Caroline Simons-Edersheim ("Tante Lin"), and Hannie Simons, in 1939 at The Hague.

The three Simons girls.

(Left to Right) Judith Révész, her mother, Magda Révész, and father Géza Révész.

Postcard of Ashley Chase, the country estate of Gustav and Thekla Broessler's hosts, Sir David and Lady Olga Milne-Watson, after the Broesslers came to England. Ruth's son, Mark Newmark, visited the estate in July 1990, fifty years after the Broesslers were labeled as "enemy aliens" and were forced to leave the area.

Eva's Third Reich passport, issued in January of 1939. Eva needed this passport when she left Vienna for The Netherlands.

Eva wearing a coat with the Star of David sewn onto it, indicating that she was a Jew.

(Left to Right) Marianne Simons-van Raalte ("Oma") and Estella C. Simons ("Tante Stel").

Johanna Simons-van Hamersveld ("Mommy" Simons) in 1940.

The Simons home in Utrecht, Koningslaan 19. Euphemia Henriette Maria Simons ("Phemia") and Estella C. Simons ("Tante Stel") are in the doorway; Eva is sitting on the second floor balcony, 1941.

Document issued to Eva during the war, granting her permission to stay in Utrecht.

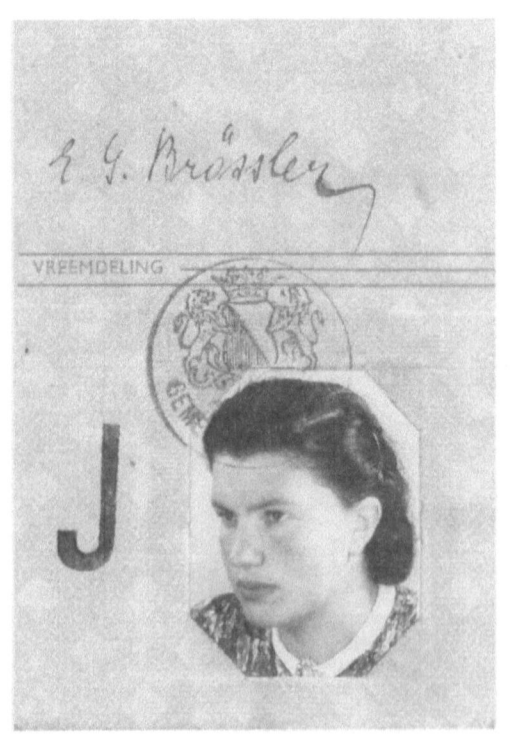

Identification card issued to Eva in Utrecht. Note the "J" identifying Eva as a Jew.

Elly and Frits Isaac in October 1942.

Eva and Ruth in Utrecht, 1942.

Marinus Simons in 1943.

Tante Lin Simons with Jewish star, August 1943.

On the right is Eva's identification card, provided by the Dutch Resistance, identifying her as Johanna Cornelia Meijer. On the left is Eva's identification card for Het Parool, *given to her when the newspaper went above ground after the war. Requiring a photograph for her card, Eva removed the photograph from her Meijer ID and affixed it to the new ID.*

Identification card issued to Eva when she worked at the censorship office after the war.

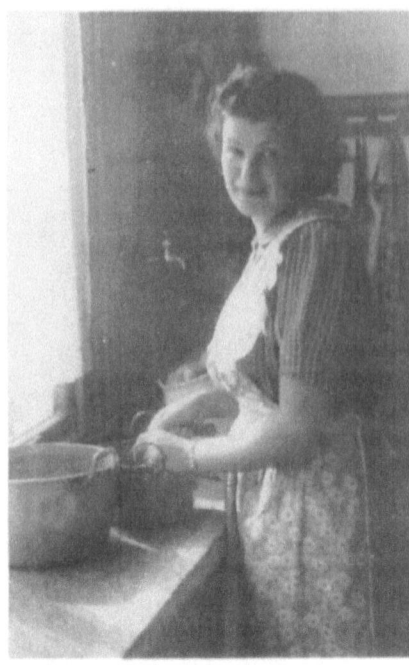

Eva in the Simons' kitchen, Amsterdam, June 1945, with half-empty pots, demonstrating that food was still in short supply even though the war had ended.

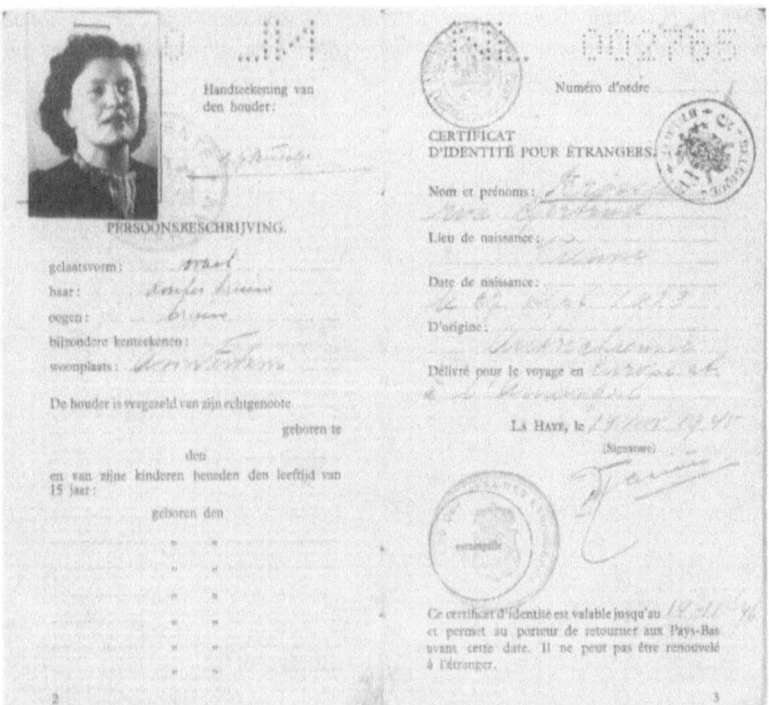

"Document for Stateless People" issued by the Dutch government to Eva. This document served as the equivalent of a passport for Eva as she received a visa to the United States.

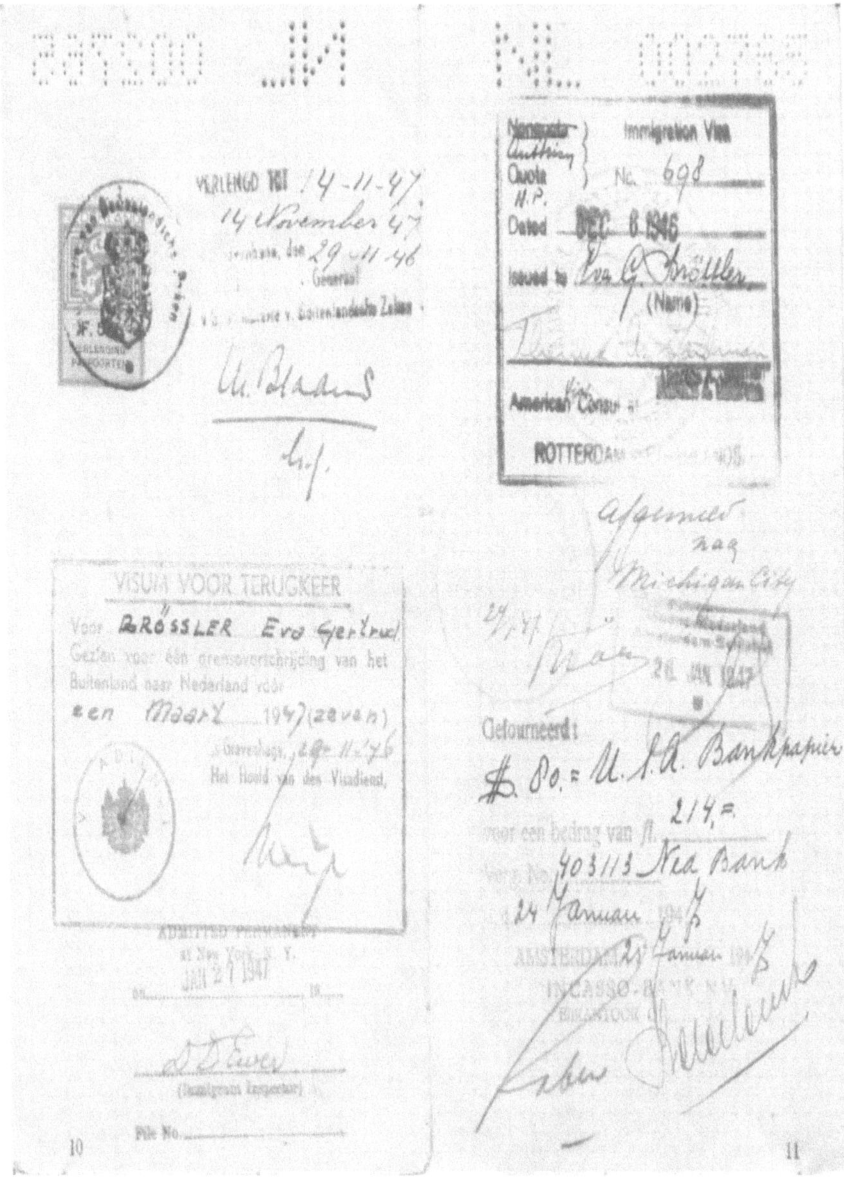

Page in Eva's stateless passport with her American visa stamped on it.

Series of photographs of Estella C. Simons ("Tante Stel") in 1948.

Peter Broessler in the U.S. Army, 1953.

Judy (Judy Beth) and Andy (L. Andrew) Weissman in December 1956.

I. Oscar Weissman, MD, MPH, in 1959.

I. Oscar Weissman, MD, MPH, in 1959.

Eva in London, 1968.

Eva as Field Director for the National Council of Jewish Women, New York City, 1969.

Eva's cousin Trude, her daughter Linda Lasner, and son Daniel Lasner at Linda's graduation from Villanova University (Villanova, Pennsylvania), in May 1986.

Eva and Hansi (Engl) Kennedy in front of Sigmund Freud's home in London, on a trip taken during the 1990s. Hansi Kennedy was trained in psychoanalysis by Sigmund's daughter, Anna, and succeeded her as co-director of the Hempstead Child Therapy Clinic in London.

Eva and Ruth with Miep Gies, the preserver of Anne Frank's diary, in the home of Euphemia ("Phemia") Simons, Amsterdam, 1996.

"A Life With a View," an illustration made by Ruth's daughter, Katya Newmark, for Eva's birthday in 1998.

Ruth's 70th birthday celebration at the home of Arthur and Carla Isaac in Amsterdam, July 2001. Top (Left to Right) Euphemia Henriette Maria Simons ("Phemia"), Sophie Marianne Simons ("Jobje"), Jobje's husband Herman van den Bergh, and Judith Simons ("Tin") Gompen; Bottom (Left to Right) Arthur Isaac toasting Ruth, Benjamin Isaac, and Ruth's husband Leonard Newmark.

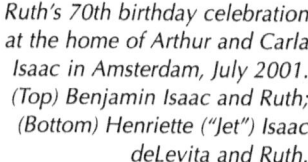

Ruth's 70th birthday celebration at the home of Arthur and Carla Isaac in Amsterdam, July 2001. (Top) Benjamin Isaac and Ruth; (Bottom) Henriette ("Jet") Isaac deLevita and Ruth.

Eva with the Newmark family in La Jolla, California, in 2001 (Left to Right) Katya, her husband Matthew Costello, Eva, Danya Costello, Leonard Newmark, Ruth, Justin Costello, and Mark Newmark.

Eva and Ruth in 2001.

The nameplate for the villa at Severin Schreibergasse 1, one of the places where the Broessler family lived in Vienna, taken during a family trip to Austria in 2008.

The villa at Severin Schreibergasse 1, one of the places where the Broessler family lived in Vienna, taken during a family trip to Austria in 2008.

Eva with staff members of her school, the Billrothgymnasium, during her visit to Vienna in 2008.

Chapter Four

Ruth's Escape

The Isaacs, with whom Ruth was living, had begun planning their escape from Holland soon after the deportations began in July 1942 and before Eva's identity change. It was beginning to be known that deportation to a concentration camp in Poland meant death. Even the children were aware of this. For Frits Isaac, the moment that sparked his decision to try to escape with his family and Ruth had come a month earlier, in June 1942, when the German forces in North Africa had captured Tobruk, and it had become clear that even if the Allies were to win the war, it would not be in the near future.[1]

It was also at about this time that the Germans announced the conscription of Dutch Jews for transportation to the so-called "labor camps" in the East. On three occasions the Isaacs were nearly included in the round-ups that began in July. On one occasion, a pair of Dutch policemen who were associated with the deportations came to the Isaacs' house, apparently to arrest them. Jet, who was about to leave for school, was sarcastically told that she would not have to worry about going to school any more. Frits managed to convince the duo to allow him to call his wife's brother, Henri Edersheim, who was a member of the Jewish Council. Edersheim had good relations with the head of the German administration at The Hague, Franz Fischer, whom he called immediately for help after speaking with Frits. Edersheim explained to Fischer that the Isaac family was protected by the Jewish Council as Elly was trustee of a Jewish orphanage and Frits was likewise entitled to special consideration through his membership in an important Jewish cultural organization. Through Edersheim and Fischer's intervention the Isaac family avoided arrest and deportation. The family would go into hiding on two other occasions. One time would be the result of a false alarm, but on the second occasion the family members went into hiding for about a week. The family was forced to scatter, with each member going into seclusion with a different Gentile friend before they were reunited once the immediate danger had passed.[2]

Frits had learned that escape might be possible as he had become aware of rumors circulating among a group of eastern European Jews who had escaped from their homelands and had settled in The Netherlands. These stories had gradually spread to a broader segment of the Jewish population. A friend, by the name of Thalheimer, had escaped to Brussels, but had advised Frits that the journey had been far more dangerous than he had anticipated.

Frits feared that escaping from Nazi-occupied territory was riskier than he had originally thought. When the man who had helped Thalheimer escape showed up in Amsterdam again in September, and was passing the word that escape was again possible, Frits decided that this connection was not sufficiently trustworthy and he began to explore other alternatives. Eventually, he made new contacts within the Dutch underground, some of whom he also dismissed as unreliable. Frits then approached Jonkheer (Squire) Belaerts van Blokland, a man who not only had a Jewish wife but who also was acquainted with many of the Isaacs' friends. Van Blokland proved to be the dependable connection to the illegal underground movement that would help them to escape to Switzerland. Preparations for the dangerous journey were begun; preparations that were made all the more difficult by the fact that the Isaacs, like all Jews in The Netherlands now, could not legally use any form of transportation, could not be in the homes of non-Jews, and did not even have a telephone, since theirs, like all telephones that had belonged to Dutch Jews, had been confiscated.[3]

While they were not told of the planned escape, the children sensed something was happening. Despite their curiosity, they did not ask questions, understanding that it was dangerous to do so. The flight cost the Isaacs a veritable fortune, "an unbelievable sum of money," as Ruth put it. For even one or two persons to try and flee from occupied territory would have been difficult enough; for a family of five to make such an attempt was incredibly dangerous. Not only would the family members be at risk, but so would all of the Resistance members who would have to take part in such an enterprise. The obstacles to overcome were equally daunting. False papers would be needed for all of them, a route to their eventual destination would have to be worked out, guides (known as *passeurs*) would have to be found, methods of transportation chosen, and safe houses had to be located. Members of the Resistance would escort Ruth and her foster family all the way to Switzerland, selflessly sharing the hazards of the journey with them. Each *passeur* was with them for just a portion of the trip, guiding them along that part of the escape route that he was familiar with. The children had to be cautioned to keep quiet so that any people they encountered would not realize that they did not speak the local language.[4]

To accomplish all of this would be extremely expensive. Some time afterward, Ruth learned that the price of their escape was equivalent to the cost of a large house the Isaacs had been building in Amsterdam. The actual cost was 50,000 Dutch guilders, a sum that was agreed to after negotiations with the Resistance. The problem for the Isaacs was how to come up with that much money when all of their assets had been confiscated by the Nazis. Frits turned to a friend on the Bijenkorf board of directors, Dick de Jong, who agreed to help. De Jong managed the Ketjen chemical manufacturing company, and he came up with the cash by siphoning off a day's worth of income from the chemical factory. Instead of producing the usual oil related product they normally made, the factory clandestinely made saccharin on that particular day, and De Jong sold it on the black market. He then loaned the cash to Frits to pay for their escape attempt. (Indeed, the loan was fully repaid after the war.)[5]

While all of this was happening, Eva went underground. The Isaacs were aware of Eva's situation, as word had been sent to them. Frits knew where she was and Ruth understood that her sister had gone into hiding. Shortly before they left The Netherlands, Frits met with Eva and told her the family was about to flee to Switzerland. Frits felt that Eva could not go with them, because an escape attempt with five people, three of whom were young children, was difficult enough. Adding Eva to the group would have only increased the risk that much more.[6]

Their escape began at six in the morning on November 1, 1942. Ruth and the Isaacs quietly left their house in The Hague. Taking nothing more than the clothes on their backs, including a double set of underwear for warmth, they made their way to the railroad station. The clothes they wore were without the required yellow star. They were all poorly dressed in the hope that they would be taken for a worker and his family.[7]

The family boarded a train that would take them to the town of Roosendaaal, close to the Belgian border. There, they would meet a member of the Dutch Resistance, a guide who would serve as their passeur to Antwerp. The arrival in Roosendaaal was not without incident, however. Their passeur nearly missed the rendezvous as he stopped for a glass of beer and lost track of time.

The real concern, however, was Ruth. She had come down with a case of foot eczema two weeks before their scheduled departure, and she was still unable to walk very far. The Isaacs, therefore, had arranged for a second passeur, a medical student and the leader of the entire expedition, to meet them when the train arrived. He arrived ahead of the other passeur, who showed up a bit later. The medical student would take Ruth across the Belgian border on the back of his bicycle, while the other passeur and the Isaacs walked across the border. All of them would meet at a designated time once they arrived in

Antwerp. Everyone, of course, was traveling under false papers; Ruth journeyed into Belgium under the name Sylvia de Boer.[8]

The plan worked, after a fashion. Ruth and her guide arrived in Antwerp without incident and settled in to wait for the others. The rest took longer than expected to make the trip. Although the Isaacs had started out by taxi, they ended up walking for several miles through secluded fields in order to cross into Belgium undetected. When they failed to arrive at the appointed time, Ruth and the passeur with her became apprehensive. As the hours crawled by, Ruth became so frightened that her foster family had been captured that she could not eat or drink. Her passeur did all he could to keep Ruth's spirits up, but it was clear that he, too, was concerned that the others had been caught by the Nazis and that he might have to take Ruth back to The Netherlands. But, after several hours of agonized waiting, the Isaacs and their escort finally arrived at the meeting place. Ruth was overjoyed to see her foster family again, and would later say as she remembered the journey that she was so relieved that "my heart began to beat again."

From Antwerp, the small band made their way to Brussels. The city looked strange to them, because, unlike in The Netherlands where strict blackouts were the rule, nighttime Brussels was brightly lit. The travelers boarded a streetcar that would take them to their next destination. There were a number of German soldiers on the streetcar, which undoubtedly added to the tension Ruth and the Isaacs must have been under, and they were nearly separated once again. None of them knew exactly where they were going, for if they were captured they could not reveal the address of the safe house that was to be their refuge for the next few days. Riding on a streetcar filled with German troops to an unknown destination made that leg of the journey especially nerve-wracking.[9]

The weary travelers arrived at a large house packed with other illegals, among them refugees like themselves. There were also non-Jewish members of the underground and an English soldier Ruth describes as a "parachutist" who was trapped behind enemy lines. Here they would stay for a while until new documents could be prepared for them. Now Ruth and the Isaacs would have to travel under Belgian papers, which, of course, were forged. Ruth, who had been "Sylvia de Boer" during the first leg of the journey, would now become a Belgian girl named "Sylvia de Laet," residing in Rue de Jemappes in Wavre. It was unfortunate that Wavre is located in the French-speaking part of the country, while the children spoke no word of French. Their new papers, however, were valid not only for travel in Belgium but also for the German-occupied part of France.[10]

On the evening before their planned departure, several Resistance fighters were captured on the street near the safe house. One of them, the medical student (Henk Pelser, whose name Ruth did not yet know), was able to escape. He came to the safe house to warn everyone that they would have to leave as soon as possible as it was likely that the Germans had learned the location of the safe house. No one could leave before morning, since there was an enforced curfew; anyone on the streets before six o'clock in the morning would most likely be arrested. Ruth, the Isaacs and the other occupants of the safe house spent an anxious night before departing as soon as the curfew was lifted the next morning. Slipping out through a cellar exit, the Isaacs and Ruth joined another couple and left for the train station at six. They would learn afterwards that the Germans had searched the safe house about two hours later, finding nothing but an empty building.

By then Ruth and the Isaacs were well on their way toward the French border. They traveled by train and bus to Bouillon, in southern Belgium. Here they spent the afternoon in a café waiting for nightfall. It was dark when the fugitives left Bouillon, traveling by taxi on roads that wound through the Ardennes Forest to the French border. They easily passed inspection by the border guards. They were merely asked, *"Avez vous quelque chose à declarer?"* ("Do you have anything to declare?") Replying for all of them, their passeur responded, *"Rien que l'amour."* ("Nothing but love.") This was clearly an arranged password, and the escapees were ushered through the border between Belgium and France without incident. Ruth is still amazed that they were not caught. At that time, she was eleven, Arthur was ten, and Jet twelve.[11]

Now in France, the party arrived in Sedan, which still bore the scars of destruction inflicted upon it by the Germans during the May 1940 invasion. They looked for somewhere to sleep, but not much was available. Ruth and Jet shared a room in a shabby hotel, which was filled with drunken revelers who sang and shouted throughout the night, so that the two girls, despite being exhausted and hungry, got very little rest. They had not eaten in hours; they were worn out and under enormous strain.

After a fearful and sleepless night, Ruth, the Isaacs, and their two passeurs boarded a local train for the city of Nancy. Once again Frits and Elly reminded the children not to talk in order to avoid calling attention to the fact they were not French speakers. Understanding their peril, the children did as they were told and kept silent. They arrived safely in Nancy and spent the night at the Hotel Jeanne d'Arc, which was located in the Rue Jeanne d'Arc.[12]

The plan was to spend one day in Nancy, then depart on November 7 for a small village near the frontier, accompanied all the while by the same couple that had brought them from Brussels. A different passeur who knew the terrain would then get them safely across the border into Switzerland. The following morning, after a restful night, the family and their guides continued by train to the village of Lure, near the French/Swiss border. The refugees reached the village safely, but the next passeur failed to make the arranged rendezvous. Later the family learned that the guide had become frightened and had returned home. They waited in vain at the train station for most of the day, growing more concerned with every passing hour. Because of the village's proximity to the Swiss border, the Gestapo conducted regular sweeps for fugitives, so that it was too dangerous to stay. Finally, Frits and Elly decided that the best thing to do would be to return to Nancy where they would try to reestablish contact with the French Resistance. Adding to the sense of disappointment was the fact that it was Jet's thirteenth birthday, which they had all hoped to celebrate in Switzerland.[13]

Back in Nancy, the passeurs who had taken them to Lure told them that they had to return to Brussels. Not knowing where else to go, the Isaacs decided there was nothing left to do but to return to the Hotel Jeanne d'Arc. The owner of the establishment was reluctant to take them back because every time he harbored fugitives his risk of being discovered and shot increased. Happily, his wife intervened and insisted that he give the Isaacs and Ruth shelter. She would prove helpful in other ways as well. But the family would have to wait until a new escort could be found to take them into Switzerland. Ruth and her foster family languished in Nancy for about a week. The five of them were crowded into a single room at the nondescript hotel until arrangements for another passeur could be made. The room they slept in had a single window, but during the daylight hours Ruth and her foster family had to move to another room that had no windows. Food was available, but in limited amounts, and the family was often fed mussels, which Ruth hated.[14]

For the most part, they remained hidden in their small, shabby room, hoping for a miracle that would get them to safety. Ruth's recollections of those nerve-racking days are of the father figure that her "Uncle" (Oom) Frits had become, teaching her to play chess to help relieve the boredom. On one occasion, however, much as Ruth and Eva had done during their layover in Cologne when they had left Vienna, the family ventured out of the hotel and went to see the famous Gates of Nancy. This was the city's best-known cultural site, the wrought-iron gates forming the entrance to the renowned Rococo Stanislas Square. As Ruth would note more than sixty-five years later, how could they not visit the most famous landmark in Nancy? Without learning, she said, life would not be worth living.[15]

Of course, the hotel room they stayed in cost money. The hotel owner had agreed to hide them, but he charged a high price for doing so. Since Dutch guilders could not be easily exchanged for local currency, Frits had smuggled a number of small diamonds out of The Netherlands in the stem of a pipe. Elly had brought some jewelry with her that she had kept hidden from the Germans. To get the money they needed, Frits did his best to sell some of the diamonds, but he soon discovered that it was easier to sell some of Elly's jewelry. Frits and Elly also discussed whether it might not be better to return to Belgium and go into hiding there. They knew that the money they could get by selling Elly's jewelry or the diamonds would soon run out if they stayed in Nancy much longer.

Fortunately, the hotelkeeper's wife came to their rescue before a decision about returning to Belgium had to be made. This good woman had been searching for a new guide who would help the family get safely across the Swiss border. After making inquiries for more than a week, she was finally contacted by the French Resistance. Arrangements were made for a new guide to conduct the Isaacs and Ruth out of Nancy.

The new guide escorted the family back to Lure. At the village, their passeur wished them good luck and explained that a pair of women would escort them on the next leg of their journey. The women, both wives of factory workers, had arranged for them to travel by truck to the village of Hérimoncourt, a village located near the Jura Mountains, from which they would embark on the final stage of their long flight to freedom. The Isaacs, Ruth, and their guides traveled in the back of an open truck on a bitterly cold and windy November day to the frontier village where they were to meet their last passeurs at nightfall.[16]

A strange event took place shortly after they arrived in Hérimoncourt. As the family was waiting to meet their guides, a young man, who appeared to be highly agitated, suddenly approached them. Claiming to be a Belgian pilot who had been shot down and brought to this area by the Resistance, he begged the Isaacs to let him travel with them as he had no money to engage a passeur on his own. After some discussion regarding the possibility that the man might be a spy for the Gestapo, the Isaacs courageously agreed to let him accompany them. Soon after, their guides for the final part of the journey appeared and the group began its trek across the mountains.[17]

The family, their new acquaintance, as well as another refugee couple from The Netherlands who had joined them in Nancy, walked for some hours in the dark of that long, raw November night, climbing mountain trails and walking along mountainous pathways. The trek through the mountains was arduous, especially so on the children. The eight of them were forbidden from talking so that the border patrol would not hear them. Everyone had to pay close attention to the trail; otherwise they risked becoming separated in the darkness, especially since they had to keep silent. At some point the young "pilot" disappeared, slipping away as mysteriously as he had appeared. Had he gone off on his own, thinking his chances of avoiding detection were better that way? Or was he a Gestapo agent who had gone off to alert the border patrol? Whether he was who he claimed to be or someone else altogether may never be known.

Finally, the small band of travelers was halted by their guides, who pointed off into the distance. *"Ici c'est la Suisse,"* they said. ("Here is Switzerland.") Carefully, the passeurs described where the family was most likely to encounter the border patrol, which would have dogs with them. The guides told them that they would have to travel the rest of the way alone. They bid the tired refugees *adieu*, and turned back. It was now around one o'clock in the morning of November 19. Exhausted, Ruth and the Isaacs picked their way over the strange terrain, moving in the direction their guides had indicated, not knowing exactly where they were and when they might actually cross into Switzerland.[18]

Since the area was patrolled by German soldiers, the Isaacs had to wait for the right moment to scurry across what they hoped was the border. After doing so, they remained uncertain as to whether or not they had left French soil and the weary group pressed on as they fought against their growing exhaustion. At last they came across a cluster of houses, which they presumed was Porrentruy, the first town they were supposed to encounter. Summoning up their courage, the family went up to one of the houses and knocked on the door. When it was answered, they asked for hospitality for the night. To their dismay, they discovered that they had chosen the home of a Swiss police officer and he was not about to give them shelter. Instead, he produced his pistol and led the Isaacs to the police station where they were detained, questioned for several hours and threatened with deportation. Elly Isaac was so distraught that she nearly collapsed, and considered taking poison. Ruth's foster parents had brought cyanide tablets with them in case they faced capture by the Nazis, preferring that they all die by their own hands rather than in a death camp in Poland. Elly feared the time to make that choice might have arrived.[19]

While they were all incarcerated and awaiting processing, they learned that they were likely to be sent back to France. The refugee couple that had joined the party at Hérimoncourt told the Isaacs that the Swiss usually gave asylum to refugees with underage children. The pair asked if they could claim Ruth as their child in order to assure gaining admittance to the country.

Frits and Elly had been presented with a terrible dilemma. If they let the couple have Ruth they might save the lives of the duo. But was it right to give up the child they had taken into their family to a pair of strangers? They didn't believe that the Swiss could be as unjust as the Germans, but, more importantly, Frits and Elly were unwilling to entrust Ruth's life to the couple, having assumed personal responsibility for her. They refused the request, and waited in the tense atmosphere of the rural police station for a decision about their fate. At last, the police made their decision. Frits was taken away to a Swiss jail, while Elly and the children were placed on a truck and delivered to a convent. The other couple, Mr. and Mrs. Adolphe Sann, were refused entry and were escorted back to France. After the war, Ruth learned to her horror that the Sanns had been captured and had lost their lives in a concentration camp in Poland.[20]

Ruth, the Isaac children and Elly remained in the convent for about a week. The nuns fed them and saw to it that they had clean beds to sleep on. The days were long, as there was little to do. Other than being allowed to get a few minutes worth of exercise in the convent yard, for most of each day "we sat and stared at the walls."[21] Elly and the children had no change of clothing and they had to bathe in ice-cold water. Since it was winter in the Jura Mountains and there was no heat, the convent cell in which they slept was bitterly cold. All of them were exhausted from the strain of their flight and were physically run down as well. And they could never be certain that they were truly safe from the Nazis since they had to wait and see if they would be allowed to remain in Switzerland or if they would be sent back to France.[22]

Elly and the children waited fearfully in the alien convent while the local gendarmerie and the national military authorities decided what to do with them. At last, the Swiss police transported them to a large refugee camp, Camp Büren, where much to their joy they were reunited with Frits. As unpleasant as the living conditions had been in the convent, they were much harsher in this international camp created for people who had fled the numerous German-occupied countries. They all slept on straw mattresses, the food was watery and distributed from large pails, and the camp was infested with lice, fleas and rats. Happily, they were in the camp only for a short period. Frits and Elly were able to contact the Dutch embassy and on December 9, the embassy staff arranged to have the family transferred to a camp for Dutch refugees located in Clarens on Lake Geneva.[23]

While it was a significant improvement over their previous accommodations, they were still in a refugee camp. The Dutch camp, however, had been set up in a former hotel, the Hotel Beau-Site, and having indoor toilets instead of stinking latrines was already a treat. Although there was a good deal of enforced order and drill, Ruth and the Isaacs were glad to be among people who spoke their language. Before long Ruth and her foster siblings, Jet and Arthur, were attending a Dutch school, one of the few Dutch schools outside of The Netherlands or its colonies. It was now December 1942, and for the first time in months Ruth and the Isaac family felt safe.[24]

Frits and Elly both remained in touch with the Dutch ambassador, and he assisted them in contacting their relatives in the United States. Fortunately, Frits had had the foresight to place some money in an American bank, and he now began to draw on that resource. Although he had an ample sum of money in the United States, he could not transfer it all to Switzerland due to government regulations and was permitted only to transfer a small amount of funds into Switzerland each month. He could, however, afford an apartment, and Frits applied for permission to leave the refugee camp. Presented with the opportunity to be relieved of the burden of paying for their upkeep, the Dutch embassy and the Swiss government approved the request. It was not until September 1943, however, about nine months later, that Ruth and her foster family were able to move into their own living quarters. She and the Isaac children were able to continue their schooling, but the family lived frugally, since as refugees they were forbidden to work. Food was rationed, living costs were high and the meager amount of money that could be transferred into their Swiss bank account was just enough to pay for a thrifty lifestyle.[25]

While their lives had improved, there were still the worries about those left behind. Frits and Elly had left many friends and relatives behind in The Netherlands, and would find few of them still alive when they returned to their homeland. For Ruth, there was a special sense of loneliness, even though she was with people who cared for her and who had kept her safe. Her parents were across the ocean in America and Ruth had no idea if and when she would see them again. Eva was still trapped in the Nazi-occupied Netherlands, unless she had been rounded up and sent off to a death camp. Perhaps she was living in hiding, perhaps she had been deported. There was no way of knowing. The time Ruth had spent with the Isaacs had made them her family, and their relatives were now her relatives too. There was the occasional letter smuggled out of Holland that made its way to Switzerland, but the news was always grim.[26]

Early in 1945, Ruth and her foster parents and siblings left the area near Montreux, where they had spent the last two years, and moved to Geneva. There the Isaacs were blessed with a new addition to the family, a baby boy they named Benjamin. Ruth recalled that the family loved and spoiled the infant, and that the children enjoyed helping Elly take care of him.[27]

Relocating to Geneva meant that Ruth would attend her eighth school in eight years. She was placed in the Ecole Internationale, an international school where the instruction was carried out in French, the primary language spoken in that part of Switzerland. Ruth now had the dual challenges of adjusting to a new school, with new schoolmates, and learning a new language. Although Ruth had been living in an area in which French was spoken, she had attended a Dutch school and had had limited contact with the French language as the Swiss children in the neighborhood were forbidden by their parents to play with the Jewish refugees.[28] At the Ecole Internationale her French improved quickly, facilitated no doubt by the fact that she was eager to communicate with her schoolmates who came from many different countries but whose mutual language of conversation was French. It helped that Ruth had the comfort of knowing she was safe and with people who cared for her. She could hope to see her parents again. But she had no way of knowing what fate might have befallen Eva.

NOTES

1. Broessler, *My Life*; Newmark, *Memoir*, 21.
2. Ibid.
3. Newmark, *Memoir*, 23.
4. Ibid.; Broessler, *My Life*.
5. Ibid.; Correspondence between Ruth Newmark and Gregory Moore, September 13, 2005; Newmark, *Memoir*, 21–22.
6. Telephone interview, Eva Weissman and Gregory Moore, February 17, 2005.
7. Broessler, *My Life*; Correspondence between Ruth Newmark and Gregory Moore, September 15, 2005.
8. Ibid.
9. Ibid.
10. Newmark to Moore, September 15, 2005.
11. Ibid.
12. Ibid.; Correspondence between Ruth Newmark and Gregory Moore, September 25, 2005.
13. Ibid.; Broessler, *My Life*.
14. Ibid.; Newmark to Moore, September 25, 2005.
15. Ibid.; Broessler, *My Life*.
16. Ibid.
17. Ibid.; Broessler, *My Life*.
18. Ibid.
19. Ibid.
20. Ibid.
21. Ibid.
22. Ibid.
23. Ibid.
24. Ibid.
25. Ibid.
26. Ibid.
27. Ibid.
28. Ibid.

Chapter Five

Hidden in Plain Sight

In Amsterdam, Eva had settled into her new life as Johanna Cornelia Meijer. She would live in Amsterdam for nearly three years, from 1942 to 1945, under her assumed identity. Life was harder in Amsterdam than it had been in Utrecht. There was less food available, and rationing was the order of the day. Since Eva was living under an assumed name, her ration card, like all of her documents, had to come from the Dutch Resistance.[1]

Hiding, or "diving under" as people referred to it, was extremely dangerous. Despite having a reputation for tolerance, The Netherlands was not free of anti-Semitic feelings. Gentiles and Jews had lived together for centuries without conflict, avoiding the violence and pogroms that had surfaced in many other European countries. What anti-Semitism that existed was usually non-violent and took the form of keeping Jews from certain institutions or offices. For most Jews this seemed to be more of a nuisance than anything else. Many Dutch Gentiles openly denounced the persecution of Jews in Germany, for example, prior to the Nazi invasion of their own land.

After the German occupation of The Netherlands, many Dutch found excuses for looking the other way once the persecution of their own Jewish population began. At first, it was easy for Dutch Gentiles to simply ignore what was happening. Later, when the persecution of Dutch Jews became more public and extreme, they started to offer excuses for not coming to the aid of their Jewish countrymen. Dutch Jews were not being killed, they argued, or things would improve once the war ended and then the Jews would be compensated for their suffering. While not all Dutchmen felt this way, there was a substantial number who seemed to be grateful that it was the Jews who were suffering and not they. It can also be argued that many people preferred not to know what was happening. They could point out their own suffering, for example, and the German policies made it easy for many Dutch to ignore the truth. Although there was some cooperation between Jews and the Resistance, as there was in other occupied countries, even some members of the Dutch Resistance had little or no sympathy for the plight of The Netherlands' Jews. Indeed, anti-Semites in the Resistance sometimes betrayed Jews to the Germans. It should also be noted that Resistance groups in some cases were reluctant to accept Jews into their organizations because they were much more exposed and likely to attract attention from the Nazis than Gentiles were. And, of course, some Dutch citizens either secretly or openly turned Jews over to the Nazis.[2]

There were also those Dutch who openly collaborated with the Germans in confiscating the property of Jews. Moving vans belonging to the A. Puls Company, owned by a Dutchman who openly worked with the Nazis, could be seen hauling away confiscated property from the Jewish sector in Amsterdam. Collaborationist military units were formed, the *Nederlandsche SS* (Dutch SS) formed in September 1940; and the *Landwacht* (Home Guard), an auxiliary police force, was created in 1941. There was also the *Vrijwilige Hulp-Police* (Volunteer Auxiliary Police), established in May 1942, tasked to help round up Jews for deportation to the death camps. Also organized that year was the *Freiwilligen Legion Niederlander* (Dutch Volunteer Legion), a military style unit that was linked to the SS.[3]

There were, of course, those who did what they could to help save lives. An official on the Jewish Council, Walter Süsskind, aided by the Resistance, smuggled Jewish infants out of a nursery. Other officials assisted fellow Jews in slipping away from various staging points in Amsterdam.

An underground organization was built by a Zionist youth group with the goal of smuggling its members to unoccupied southern France or Spain, or to help them go into hiding. With the assistance of non-Jews, the group was able to get nearly eighty of its members across the Pyrenees while approximately 240 others were able to survive by hiding. By war's end, the group had managed to save the lives of about half their members.[4]

Jews seeking to escape the round-ups had a limited number of options. One was to join the Resistance and both Jewish men and women were active in all of the branches of the Dutch Resistance, despite anti-Semitic elements within the underground. Jews in the Dutch Resistance movement took part in acts of sabotage, carried out espionage activities against the Germans, and assisted fellow Jews as they tried to escape to neutral countries. Little is known, however, about the role of Jews in the Dutch Resistance because so few survived.

Trying to escape any Nazi-occupied territory was a highly dangerous enterprise for Jews, and fleeing The Netherlands was no exception. Those who fled, such as Eva's sister Ruth and her foster family, faced many risks—the possibility of treachery and betrayal was with them every step of the way, even when there was assistance available. Those who aided Jews in their efforts to escape did so at great personal risk, of course. Always, however, the fugitives faced those times when they were completely on their own; how many actually tried to escape The Netherlands may never be known.

Flight from German-occupied territories was almost always arduous. Fugitives might have to ford a river, cross mountains, travel at night, and have to fool suspicious Nazi officials, police or guards. They might spend days in hiding often with little or no food and sleep. And they lived with the constant fear that one tiny slip, one false step, one moment of carelessness would prove fatal. Adding to the risk were those strangers who might approach Jews with an offer to help them escape — for a price, of course, which was usually expensive. Those who chose this method might actually succeed in escaping, but others were simply led right to the Nazis. Still others tried to ransom or bribe their way out of the country. Success in these endeavors was mixed as well, depending on the mood of the authorities. And there was always the danger that someone would double-cross the fleeing Jews, even if an official had been paid off.[5]

Some fled on their own; others fled in groups. Most of those who made the attempt, however, were single men (making the successful escape of Ruth and the Isaacs even more remarkable). It is estimated that some 2,000 Jews were able to successfully escape The Netherlands once the deportations began — about half the number who survived by going underground.

Many Jews, like Eva, chose (or had the choice made for them) to go underground; to "dive under" as some called it. Although many people courageously risked their own lives to help Jews hide from the Germans, the Dutch may not have been as helpful in this regard as other Europeans were.[6] Estimates as to how many actually went underground vary; some go as high as 30,000, although it is likely that the number was lower. Perhaps as many as 10,000 people in hiding were caught by the Germans, with from 8,000 to 10,000 hidden Jews surviving the war.[7]

"Diving under" meant overcoming a number of obstacles. Obviously someone had to be willing to conceal Jews who sought to go underground. Then, as Eva learned, there was the need to acquire false identity papers; these might be paid for, or they might not cost anything. These were usually acquired as persons "lost" their identity cards, allowing the fugitive to pose as the individual (which meant that one had to memorize all the details of the new identity). Having a plausible occupation was also helpful, although circumstances did not always permit that to be the case. And, depending on the occupation given on the false identity card, one might also have to carry additional documents "proving" the carrier was what he or she claimed to be.

This meant that every false document had to have the proper stamps, had to be printed on the proper paper with the correct letterheads and carry the correct signatures. Even so, these documents would not have stood up to more than a cursory inspection, meaning that they were good for little more than providing a basic cover identity that would allow the person to "hide in plain sight." In extreme cases some persons disguised themselves, wore makeup or even submitted to plastic surgery in order to create a new persona. Eva, fortunately, did not have to go to these lengths as she began her life underground.

Another challenge, which also entailed risk, was the need to move to some other part of the country as one could not safely hide in one's own neighborhood. This was one of the great hardships of going underground, as this meant abandoning one's home and possessions perhaps never to see them again. Nor was it uncommon to have to change hiding places. Some persons moved to several different shelters during their years of hiding, while others remained in just one or two places. It was not uncommon for those Dutch Jews who opted to go into hiding to move from place to place, always in danger of being exposed or betrayed every time they did so.

To help their "guests" cope with the strains of living underground, many hosts performed acts of kindness such as providing a small pet for the person to care for, or presenting them with a cake or other treat to welcome the guest into their homes. The fear and loneliness for Jews in hiding had to be great, and often their only source of human contact was with their host. Often, but not always, the host sheltered a Jewish fugitive without asking for anything in return and risked his or her life in the process.

Sheltering a Jewish fugitive was an extremely risky endeavor and the Germans made this abundantly clear to the Dutch. Warning signs were posted everywhere, the price on Jewish heads was constantly increased and those found sheltering Jews were severely punished. No hiding place was ever really safe. The neighbors might harbor anti-Semitic feelings, or even if they did not, they still might accidentally let something slip. A servant or workman might try to blackmail the host, or the postman might become suspicious.

Life was difficult for both hosts and guests alike. Children and relatives posed difficulties, for example. A "guest" might have to be concealed when the host's parents or relatives came over for a visit, since they would need to be kept ignorant of the situation for the safety of everyone. And those Jews hiding in homes with children might spend most of their time in their rooms so that the children would not know of their presence, as children were very likely to talk.

"Guests" often stayed with their hosts for years, which required a great deal of sacrifice on the part of the persons who provided shelter for Jews in hiding. Hosts often gave up things that they wanted to do since strangers were living with them, and any number of unanticipated events could take place. Even feeding a guest could be problematic. If the guest ate with the family, then the family lost time together. If the guest ate alone, then the meals had to be taken to him or her. Guests had to be fed from the family's meager rations, since the timely arrival of the guest's ration tickets, if any, could not be counted upon. And, as the war dragged on, the food situation worsened with every passing year.

Holidays were almost entirely out of the question. Even leaving the house entailed a degree of danger. So, guest and host alike found themselves forced to put up with each other daily whether or not they liked it. If both parties could be free and open with each other that may have minimized the stresses of their relationship. Often, though, relations between both parties were strained as they tried to work out the nature of what undoubtedly was an awkward relationship. Where did concern for one's guest cross the line into interference, for example? What were the limits as to what guests could and could not do? All too often the guest had to rely on the judgment of the host, who was assuming a great deal of risk to provide shelter.

From time to time guests were exploited by their hosts. Some had to pay weekly charges for their room and board, for example, and those who did not have the means to pay were in danger of being thrown out. Others might be charged exorbitant fees for ration coupons. In some cases, survivors were still paying the debts they had accrued after The Netherlands had been liberated.

Those in hiding often received assistance from many others besides those who sheltered them. Some persons served as intermediaries who arranged for a host for those seeking to go underground. Others transported fugitives to their hiding place or helped keep them in touch with the outside world. These people, like those who served as hosts, also put their lives at risk. There were some who worked as couriers, traveling from town to town in order to deliver ration cards, false documents, even letters; to deliver illegal newspapers or even to escort fugitive Jews to a new hiding place, when the old one was no longer safe.[8]

Although The Netherlands was occupied territory, and the Germans did all they could to limit the amount of knowledge the Dutch received about the war's progress, they were not able to shut off all outside sources of information. Johanna Simons had a radio hidden in her stationery shop, located high on a shelf in the store's window. During the day, the radio was concealed by a curtain. At night, when shutters covered the outside of the window, Siebert, Johanna's son, climbed up a ladder to listen to the radio, reporting what he heard to the family. The illicit radio gave Eva and the others access to BBC broadcasts, so that they could follow the Allied efforts to turn the tide of the war in their favor.[9] Nor was the hidden radio the only source of knowledge for Eva. Through exposure to other intellectuals who had been uprooted from their homes by the war, Eva was able to continue a semblance of her education.[10]

Despite her new status as an *onderduiker* (underdiver), Eva soon found that this life took on routine aspects. Having enough food to eat and keeping the apartment warm on cold nights were ongoing concerns, especially as rationing increased. Depending on how much water was available, a simple chore such as cleaning the dishes after a meal could take hours. Reading or playing cards helped pass the time and, at night, the Simons and their "guests" could listen to the BBC on Johanna's radio. Going out at night was forbidden, as the Germans had established an eight o'clock curfew and anyone found on the streets after that time was likely to be arrested. Food and coal shortages were common during the occupation, and households could never be sure what foodstuffs might be available at any time. Constant shortages drove food, commodity and coal prices up, both on the open and black markets alike. Nonetheless, life settled into a constant and tedious routine of endurance and survival.[11]

There were many moments of intense terror as well. The shop had, as noted earlier, a hiding place for Eva and the other refugees Mrs. Simons[12] sheltered. From time to time, the Gestapo conducted house to house searches for Jews and other fugitives. On one of these occasions, Eva had to hide in the cellar for several hours. Only nineteen at the time, Eva vividly recalls that occasion. She had to climb down a ladder, after which the trap door in the floor was closed and a desk was placed over it. On this particular occasion, Eva remained in this small cellar for nearly half the night.[13] To be left alone in the cellar was a terrifying experience, and Eva would later marvel that she was able to get through the ordeal. Particularly frightening was the knowledge that her only means of escape from the cellar, which she thought of as a "subterranean pit," was through the trap door that had that heavy desk resting on it. Eva naturally worried about the possibility that the Simons family could be taken away by the Gestapo, leaving her trapped below.[14]

Eva's official "disappearance" and becoming an onderduiker proved beneficial to the Dutch Resistance, although it also exposed her to additional danger. She began to help deliver *Het Parool* (*The Parole*), the underground paper published by the Resistance since 1941, door to door in Amsterdam in 1944. Eva usually went with one of the Simons girls, Jobje mostly, and, despite the risk involved, found it pleasant to be outside in the evening, especially during the spring. These deliveries were made at night, before curfew, and had Eva been caught by the authorities it would have been a certain death sentence for her. Eva later recalled that the papers were distributed "to anybody. We threw [them] in the mailbox and ran." Eva, and the others who delivered *Het Parool*, were kept unaware of the location of the illegal paper's publishing facility, most likely to prevent them from revealing the source of the underground publication to the Gestapo should they be caught. The carriers picked up the papers from various locations to further minimize their chances of being apprehended. Once each carrier had completed his or her route, leftover copies were tossed into the canals. From a historical standpoint, it is unfortunate that these papers were lost, as the records of the Dutch Resistance have gaps today that these lost copies would have helped to fill. In time, Eva expanded her activities as a courier for the Resistance and began delivering packages for them. She never knew what she might be carrying in these packages and never asked.[15]

As the war continued, conditions worsened. During the winter of 1944–1945, fuel became scarce, and to keep warm on cold nights, Eva and the others slept with hot water bottles and were glad to be able to do so as long as hot water remained available. When she and Ruth were able to exchange letters after the war's end, Eva described how the Dutch had been reduced to eating tulip bulbs and how hard it had been to endure the frostbite conditions of that winter.[16] Eva would later portray these dreary, cold, miserable years as ones of darkness, lacking in color.[17] Sixty years later, Eva recalled that eating tulip bulbs "was really not bad, but some (called Darwin tulips) were supposedly poisonous."[18]

As food became scarce, Eva, Eka and Jobje would ride bicycles as far as sixty miles into the countryside where they would barter clothes or pieces of jewelry for food. In an interview she later gave to the Shoah Foundation, Eva explained how she and Eka exchanged everything they had for food: ". . . our good clothes, everything." Eva took pride in their ability to bargain. "People say that Jews are good business people," Eva commented, "well, Jobje and I were very good when we went to the farmers and brought back cheese, grain, and sometimes something else," such as extra vegetables or marrow bones.[19] The trips were long, and they were dangerous since the girls also distributed Resistance leaflets, or carried packages from the Resistance to the farmers they did business with. Eva, Jobje and Eka risked being arrested every time they made such an excursion.[20]

Despite the dangers involved, Eva's later recollections of this time suggest they were somewhat exhilarating. For one thing, it was pleasant to be outside, riding their bicycles and meeting other people. Eva, the "Austrian girl," would later be remembered by Eka as an attractive foster sister "full of fun, plucky, charming, an expert in bartering with farmers." In this time of hunger, Eka "lost kilo after kilo and I was puffed up and hardly looked undernourished," Eva recalled later. The two girls were rather different in temperament and constitution, but on these long bicycle rides that ranged far from Amsterdam, the two "felt very much alike." Eva and Eka remained in contact after the war, and, years later, Eka often reminded Eva how, on their excursions, despite the seriousness of them and the danger, how the beauty of the countryside, whether in winter or spring, the sight of flooded dikes and sad-looking trees touched them both.[21]

Despite the difficulties and terror of those times, the Simons' home in Amsterdam became more than a mere shelter for refugees. As Eva would put it six decades afterward:

> So strong was the will to live and the repression of constant anxiety and danger that life went on in its truly abnormal but still somewhat orderly fashion. There were books to read; we learned to play bridge, and we increased our knowledge of English through the forbidden BBC radio broadcasts; yes, somehow we were carrying on tough as life was, trying to ignore the unheated rooms, the scarcity of food, fuel, former daily necessities and constant uncertainty.[22]

Gradually the war turned in favor of the Allies, and the Dutch could see signs of that. German planes had dominated the skies in the early years of the conflict; now fewer Nazi planes appeared overhead as the Allied air forces drove them from the skies. And, where radio broadcasts were available, the Dutch learned through BBC newscasts of the Allied advances. There was, by the spring of 1945, a growing expectation that liberation was only a matter of time.

Hunger had taken its toll. People looked like skeletons, although Eva was one of those whose appearance was not so drastically altered. Due to what she believes to be some sort of "genetic condition" she was "puffed up" while everyone else was emaciated: "I never looked undernourished, but I was."[23]

On May 6, 1945, British and Canadian planes dropped food and other supplies for the residents of Amsterdam; Canadian forces liberated the city shortly afterward. The end of the war brought massive celebrations, including dancing in the streets of Amsterdam. Eva, like everyone else, was struck by how young and healthy the Canadian soldiers looked, and was amazed by the Jeeps they rode in. During the occupation, those people who had bicycles considered themselves fortunate, even when the rubber tires gave out and wooden wheels had to be substituted. The Canadians also shared their rations with the Dutch, who were thankful for them after a winter of hunger and starvation. For those Jews who had remained in Amsterdam, liberation also brought the tragic news that so many of their people had been brutally murdered. Although it was known that the Jews who had been transported from The Netherlands and other parts of Europe had been placed in concentration camps, the full extent of the horrors that had taken place in them now came to light. Some family members, other relatives, and friends had been deported from Vienna, Budapest, Prague and elsewhere to die in the camps. Eva eventually learned of the deaths of her foster parents, Marinus and Caroline Simons, and many other relatives of both the Simons and Isaac families and their relations elsewhere. Marinus and Caroline had perished in Bergen-Belsen; however two of their children, Hannie and Tin, had survived Auschwitz and other camps. Like so many other survivors, they would wear the tattoos of their concentration camp numbers on their arms for the rest of their lives. The oldest sister had been an onderduiker with Eva after a narrow escape from the Dutch camp Westerbork. There was other good news as well. Immediate members of the Broessler family had survived, notably Eva's Uncle Otto, her Aunt Mitzi (Maria) and their children, Trude and Peter, Eva's cousins. Somehow, despite their own hardships in Vienna, they had managed to scrape enough food and other necessities together to send to Marianne and Estella Simons at Theresienstadt, a camp/ghetto near Prague. These were the women with whom Eva had lived in Utrecht from 1940 until her arrest in 1942. Sadly, Marianne died soon after her return to Utrecht. Estella returned to find everything—her home and her law practice—completely gone. Nonetheless, at the age of 57, she began the process of rebuilding her life and lived to the age of 100. Eva's foster sister Jobje, Hannie and Tin's older sister, began to adjust to postwar life. She and her sisters were now orphans, haunted by the thoughts of the deaths of their parents in a concentration camp, and forced to face their own future without parental guidance. And Eva, along with her Viennese cousins, Peter and Trude, had been robbed of their youth and formal education by the war.[24]

Despite the terrors and the suffering under the Nazi yoke, some comfort regarding the human condition could be found. There was the knowledge that so many people had risked their lives to save Jews, and it was because of people like these that Eva and others who had successfully been hidden or escaped were still alive. And, despite the horrors and hardships of the war, the survivors had gained lifelong friendships and an invaluable appreciation for life.[25]

NOTES

1. Weissman, *Life*.
2. Presser, 325–328; Warmbrunn, 170–171.
3. HC, 413, 203, 214, 318, 248.
4. Warmbrunn, 170.
5. Presser, 283–289; Warmbrunn, 170.

6. Presser, 382.
7. Presser, 383.
8. Presser, 382–391.
9. Weissman, *Life*.
10. Ibid.
11. Hans Cramer, in his "Letter from The Netherlands," describes the worsening market conditions, rising prices and constant shortages.
12. Although referred to by her name here, for those who were sheltered by Johanna she would always remain "Mommy" Simons. Eva has noted that whenever she thinks of Johanna, it is not by her given name but as "Mommy."
13. The amount of time Eva spent in the cellar on this occasion may not have been as long, perhaps two or three hours, as she recounts in her *Shoah* interview. Weissman, *Life*.
14. Ibid.; Weissman, *Shoah*.
15. Weissman, *Shoah*; Weissman, *Life*.
16. Broessler, *My Life*.
17. Weissman, *Shoah*, Weissman, *Life*.
18. Correspondence between Eva Weissman and Gregory Moore, June 14, 2005.
19. Weissman, *Shoah;* Eva Weissman interview with Gregory Moore, September 22, 2005.
20. Ibid.; Weissman, *Life*.
21. Correspondence between Eva Weissman and Gregory Moore, March 16, 2005.
22. Ibid.
23. Weissman, *Shoah*.
24. Ibid.; Weissman, *Life*; Eva Weissman, "The War Came to Me," unpublished notes on her postwar life from 1945–1946 (hereafter "The War Came to Me").
25. Eva Weissman interview, the *Cleveland Jewish News*, January 1, 1996; Weissman, "The War Came to Me."

Chapter Six

Reunions

The war's end brought both hope and problems. For the first time in nearly three years, Eva was able to communicate with her sister. Ruth "cried with joy" when she received the first letter from Eva in the summer of 1945 and learned that her sister, too, had survived the war. In subsequent letters, Eva described her life underground.[1] Eva also heard from her parents, with whom she had been unable to communicate for most of the war years. While they were aware of Ruth and her foster family's many narrow escapes and eventual arrival in Switzerland, they had lost touch with Eva altogether once she went underground. Now, through Dutch relatives, they learned that Eva, too, had survived the war and they immediately sent her a telegram expressing their joy at learning she was still alive. Letters soon followed, as did care packages filled with all kinds of treats and necessities, including clothes. These were especially welcome as it took weeks for the Dutch to get food rationing organized, although soup kitchens had opened and they provided some level of nourishment. Getting food or other necessities required having proper documentation and hours of tedium standing in line. But, as Eva noted, this was certainly not life threatening as mere survival efforts had been during the war.[2]

Although the war had ended there were new difficulties to overcome. Eva and Ruth naturally looked forward to being reunited with their parents. The sisters had learned back in 1940 of their parents' emigration from England to the United States, and that they had eventually settled in Michigan City, Indiana. Communications by mail had continued until the Japanese attack on Pearl Harbor in December 1941. Gustav and Thekla remained in Michigan City during the war since their address in that city was the last one their daughters had, and they hoped that if Eva and Ruth survived it would be easier for the girls to find them if they stayed there. The thought of joining her parents in America filled Eva with conflicting emotions. The end of the war had brought about a sense both of joy and sadness and a new sense of separation anxiety as she considered parting with the Simons family, as well as with the Révész family, with whom she had been in close touch with throughout the harrowing war years. There was the exciting thought of beginning a new life, but that was tempered by the realization that once again Eva would have to start over in a new country with a different language. She felt unprepared for what was to come. And, as much as she wanted to be reunited with her parents, Eva was filled with uncertainty about how what would be a mutual readjustment for all of them would turn out.[3]

Early in 1945, Gustav and Thekla had become citizens of the United States, and that would work to Ruth's advantage. Ruth was now fourteen, and as the minor child of American citizens she could emigrate to the U.S. without being subject to quota restrictions. Eva, however, who was now an adult, would have to enter the United States subject to the immigration quota for Austrian nationals, which meant she would have to have a number assigned to her and wait for permission to enter the country. Although both daughters would have their entry into the United States delayed, it was Ruth who was first reunited with their parents.[4]

War's end soon led to Ruth's parting from her foster family. Frits was anxious to be repatriated to Holland in order to begin rebuilding the family business. He and his brothers were major stockholders in three department stores, in Amsterdam, The Hague, and Rotterdam, with Frits serving as the CEO of the business. The stores in The Hague and Rotterdam, which had been destroyed by the German bombardment of that city, needed to be rebuilt; merchandise to sell needed to be found. Frits was able to arrange to leave for Amsterdam in July 1945; the rest of the family would join him in August. Saying goodbye to Frits was hard for Ruth; she loved her "uncle" like a father, and she was grateful for all that he had done for her.[5]

Before leaving, Frits had made arrangements for Ruth's reunion with her parents. Expecting that she would be able to leave Switzerland in September, Frits had left Ruth in the care of a Dutch minister and his Swiss wife in Klosters, a village in the German-speaking region of the country. They owned a large chalet, part of which they rented out to boarders, most of whom were Dutch. While she was well cared for, Ruth felt "totally alone" although regular letters from her parents, foster parents and Eva helped her with her loneliness.[6]

When September 1945 arrived, Ruth learned that she would not be leaving Switzerland just yet, due to a lack of transportation. The plan had been to have Ruth return to The Netherlands and sail for the United States on a passenger ship, but these vessels were being used primarily to take American troops back home. There seemed to be no chance of getting a reservation on a passenger liner and Ruth undoubtedly was frustrated with her inability to secure passage on one. In every letter her parents tried to reassure Ruth and they told her how hard they were working to get her out of Switzerland. Finally, one letter brought welcome news. Gustav and Thekla had been able to book a flight for Ruth to the United States from Amsterdam. This would afford Ruth the chance to see Eva again before she left to be reunited with their parents.[7] But new problems arose. The papers granting Ruth permission to enter the United States had expired, and they had to be renewed. Bureaucratic delays would keep Ruth in Switzerland for several more months.

The new year of 1946 began with a surprise in the form of a long-distance telephone call from Eva. The sisters were both so excited they hardly knew what to say to each other, and the few minutes allotted for the duration of the call passed all too quickly. Ruth, however, was still waiting to leave for America and she was feeling both frustrated and guilty. Her lodging at the chalet was costing her parents and Frits the equivalent of $125 a month, and Ruth felt bad about the expense. Appeals for help to the Jewish Refugee Committee in Zurich had produced no results, and finally, after Easter had come and gone, fourteen-year-old Ruth decided to take matters into her own hands. She began to make frequent calls to the American Consulate and, sometimes, to the Jewish Refugee Committee as well. At first Ruth's entreaties were ignored and she was counseled to be patient until a new visa could be issued. Ruth continued to press, however, and she was eventually called to Zurich to see the physician employed by the American Consulate. Immigration regulations required every immigrant to undergo a thorough physical examination before being admitted to the United States. Ruth arranged an appointment with the consulate's doctor who examined her thoroughly and gave her a clean bill of health. A few days later Ruth received her visa, which was given to her with the compliments of the American Consul, who commended her for being "so smart and full of energy." Now, all Ruth had to do was get to Amsterdam.[8]

Money had been deposited by Ruth's parents with the Jewish Refugee Committee to pay for her transportation to the Netherlands. The committee informed Ruth, however, that it could take as long as three months to get an airline ticket. Ruth hid her disappointment, which must have been great, and gave her parents no inkling of her frustration at being unable to begin the journey that would reunite them all. Ruth's letters to her parents remained cheerful, and the missives she received from Gustav and Thekla in return were equally so.[9] The desire to see each other again must, by now, have been overwhelming for Ruth and her parents.

Doggedly, Ruth began making the rounds of the airline offices. She encountered a variety of attitudes, from friendliness to rudeness, but Ruth was determined to begin the first leg of her journey, and to see the sister she had been separated from for more than three years. The final straw occurred when Ruth received word that Frits could no longer send her money to cover her expenses in Switzerland, due to currency regulations, and that the financial burden would now have to be borne completely by her parents. Ruth began to tell the Swiss officials that she could not remain in Switzerland any longer since she now had no one to support her. Whether this argument broke the bureaucratic logjam, or whether it was just by coincidence, within a few days Ruth obtained an airline booking to Amsterdam.[10]

Finally, in the afternoon of May 18, 1946, a year after the end of the war and about nine months after her foster family had returned home, Ruth boarded a plane for Amsterdam. The flight over the mountains was a rough one as the plane was bounced around by turbulence, but three and a half hours after takeoff the flight landed safely. Waiting to greet Ruth were Eva and the Isaac family. Eva undoubtedly barely recognized Ruth, who had been a little girl when she last saw her; now Ruth was an adolescent of about the same age Eva had been when the two girls had fled Vienna. The sisters enjoyed three weeks together. Ruth lived with Eva at the home of the Simons family during her stay, as the Isaacs' house was filled with relatives who had survived the death camps.[11]

Getting Ruth an airline reservation to the United States proved to be much easier than getting her on a plane out of Switzerland had been. A family friend of the Broesslers worked for one of the American airlines, and his influence made acquiring a plane ticket fairly simple as compared to all that Ruth had gone through back in Switzerland. Time passed quickly during Ruth's three weeks in Amsterdam, and before she knew it, the time had come for her to depart for the United States and end her long separation from Gustav and Thekla.[12]

The twenty-two hour flight to New York began on June 7. Eva and all of the Simons plus the Isaacs escorted Ruth to the airport and waved goodbye as her plane left the ground. Ruth recalls not being afraid to make the long flight across the Atlantic Ocean. The plane carried 37 passengers and a crew of five, some of whom were U.S. soldiers returning home. A few of them had brought dogs with them, and they barked incessantly during the flight. Although the flight was exhausting, Ruth was too excited to sleep. The plane stopped to refuel twice, first in Ireland and then in Newfoundland. The plane landed around 6 p.m. in Ireland and the crew and passengers were treated to a lavish meal, Ruth's first American dinner. They were all impressed with the service and luxury they enjoyed. After an hour's layover, the flight resumed and the passengers settled in for the next leg of the journey. Around midnight they arrived at a primitive airstrip in Newfoundland where "a supper and many drinks" were served. Ruth, probably too tired and excited to eat any more, did not partake of this meal. This stop, too, lasted for an hour or so before the plane took to the air again. Sunrise found the aircraft nearing the United States, and when the passengers finally were able to look down and see the Statue of Liberty everyone cheered.[13]

Ruth entered the United States on June 8, 1946, nearly seven and a half years after she and Eva had fled Austria. Ruth, naturally, was very happy to be on American soil and her happiness was intensified by the sight of her mother and father, along with a pair of uncles and aunts and a cousin, all waiting for her. Ruth was overwhelmed by joy at seeing them after so many years, although at this point she could do no more than wave to them as they were separated by a wire fence. Ruth still had three hours of processing to endure before she could feel the arms of her mother and father holding her close after all the years of separation. At last Ruth was cleared to enter the country and she rushed to her parents and kissed them for the first time in more than seven years.[14]

The family spent an exciting week in New York City. Ruth was taken on sight-seeing tours and she stared up in awe at the skyscrapers, visited Radio City Music Hall and Times Square, and took two automobile rides around the city. There were presents to open and Ruth went shopping with her mother and aunts, a necessity since she had arrived in America literally with an empty suitcase because she had outgrown all of her clothes.[15]

The family left by train for Indiana on June 17. Ruth, of course, was filled with curiosity about the city where her parents had lived for most of the last half dozen years. The train took them as far as South Bend, where they were met at the station by a friend, Herbert Levin, who drove them to Michigan City. They arrived on a Sunday, and Ruth was both joyful and thankful to have a real home again. At the same time, her first summer in America was not as pleasant as Ruth had hoped it would be. She had looked forward to swimming in Lake Michigan and doing all sorts of other fun things, but the strain of the previous years, especially her last one in Europe, had finally taken their toll on Ruth. She spent most of the summer months in the house, under a doctor's care, as she had contracted a mild case of polio. This made her assimilation into American life slower than it might have been otherwise. Despite the setbacks, she began her study of English. In mid-July her parents hired a tutor who worked with Ruth through the end of August. Both her health and English improved, and Ruth was able to begin school in September. She was disappointed that she had lost a year of schooling since it took so long to get out of Switzerland, but Ruth adjusted quickly and soon became comfortable with her new teachers and fellow students, and ultimately graduated with her agemates.[16] Like Gustav and Thekla, Ruth was anxious for the day when Eva would come home and they would all be together again.

That day would not arrive until early 1947. Besides being subject to immigration restrictions because she was an adult, Eva's return was further delayed by the American emphasis on bringing the troops home from Europe as quickly as possible. Eva remained in Amsterdam where she had briefly gone to work for *Het Parool*, which had emerged from the underground to begin publication as a daily newspaper.[17]

The restoration of mail service was soon followed by the return of telephone service and Eva began to receive calls from her Uncle Otto back in Vienna. Otto Broessler tried to persuade her to return to Vienna to live with his family while she awaited her visa to the United States. Eva realized that Otto was trying to make it possible for her to get a *Realgymnasium* certificate that would indicate she had satisfied the final requirements for graduation. Doing so would mean that Eva could enter the United States with the equivalent of two years of college education and that she might then have the opportunity to complete her formal education there. Eva had reason to believe the Viennese school system might have been generous in helping her make up for all of the years she had missed at the Realgymnasium, but she decided to turn down the opportunity: "At that point my only plan was to get to America and let the chips fall as they might."[18]

In May of 1945, Eva found a position in the Dutch Censorship Office sorting papers left behind by the Germans. She learned of the position from an advertisement in the Amsterdam newspaper. She went to apply and was hired immediately because people were needed who were fluent in German and who could censor correspondence that the Germans had left when they withdrew from The Netherlands. As Eva put it, she "sorted through old mail that was left behind." But it was more than that. On one occasion Eva discovered information describing the transport of valuable Dutch machinery to Germany. The machinery was recovered and the Netherlands was spared a significant loss. The find became Eva's "claim to fame" as a censor, a job she enjoyed doing. Eva worked as a censor until September 1945.[19]

The censorship office Eva worked in was located in the building belonging to the upscale clothing store, *Geb. Hirsch & Cie.* on *Leidsche Plein* that before the war had been owned by relatives of the Isaac, Simons and Edersheim families. The office was within easy walking distance from the *P.C. Hooftstraat*, where Eva still lived with the Simons family, so that she was saved the cost of transportation. She also began to supplement her income from the censorship office by selling American cigarettes on the black market. Setting aside her fear of the authorities, and with the assistance of her parents who sent her cartons of cigarettes, Eva was able to sell them clandestinely. Cigarettes were, as Eva would say decades later, not legal tender, but the best "currency" available. A "brief appearance at a certain place and money was in your hands fast. I don't know who looked the right way or the wrong way, but we got away with it." This was pretty much tolerated by the authorities.[20]

The money she made through these transactions would eventually help pay for her first airplane ride. Much of her time was focused on getting her visa so that she could finally leave Amsterdam for the United States or simply in getting by from day to day. Eva did break up the monotony of existence in postwar Amsterdam, however, by traveling whenever she could. She would visit friends and foster family in Utrecht and The Hague, often hitchhiking to get to her destination. She usually got rides from Canadian soldiers who not only gave her a free ride but helped her send letters to her parents through the military mail.

Then, one day, Eva was contacted by a former friend from her Viennese school days, Rita Spitzmann. Although her father had perished, Rita, along with her mother and brother, had survived the war hidden in Belgium. Rita discovered that Eva was in Amsterdam and traveled there twice to visit with her former schoolmate. She also invited Eva to visit her and her remaining family in Brussels. Eva took her first airplane ride in April 1946, flying from "a small burgeoning airport at Schiphol near Amsterdam (now a thriving international hub) to an equally unimpressive barracks-like airport in Brussels in a small propeller aircraft."[21]

Eva took pleasure in shopping for some souvenirs to take home to her Dutch saviors, the Simons family. She noted that there was more food available in Brussels than in Amsterdam and that there was more of what she thought of as "normal activity" in Belgium as compared to The Netherlands. Eva had one more reminder of her postwar status as well. The travel documents she carried during her Belgian vacation identified her as a stateless person who had been given permission to travel in and out of The Netherlands for only a short time.

Cultural activities slowly returned to Amsterdam, as they did throughout Europe. Foreign films were especially popular, as well as affordable, and Eva spent many evenings at the movies. She saw *Of Mice and Men, Mrs. Miniver, Casablanca, Gone With the Wind* and many other films that had been popular in the United States during the war years. Eva was also able to attend concerts at the Amsterdam *Concertgebouw*. As there was still little fuel available for heat in fall and winter of 1945–1946, theaters and concert halls were often rather chilly. Eva recalls one concert where the orchestra members had to put on gloves before they could begin to warm up.

Standing in line was a constant postwar activity, whether one was buying food or concert tickets. Being in line resulted in the development of life-long friendships, however. On two occasions, while waiting in line, Eva met a young woman of about her age, who, like her, was dressed a bit nicer than most of those in line. Both were wearing clothes and shoes that had obviously been made in the United States. Noticing each other's shoes, they began to talk and soon learned that they shared a similar past. Both of them had been *"onderduikers"* in Amsterdam; the other girl, whose name was Ivonne Kray, had been born in Berlin. Like Eva, Ivonne was awaiting an immigration visa to the United States. By coincidence and through mutual Dutch friends, the two women were reunited shortly after arriving in America. They greeted each other with a simultaneous outburst: "the shoes!" Eva and Ivonne Kray (Sokolow) have remained friends ever since, a testament to what Eva calls "the many unforgettable linkages of life!"[22]

Eva's visa finally came through. On January 26, 1947, she flew—like Ruth, via Ireland and Newfoundland—to New York City, arriving the next day. She was met there by her mother, who had traveled to New York by train from Michigan City to meet her. The reunion was not an entirely joyous one. Eva's feelings were somewhat uncertain, at least in part because she had left Vienna and her parents as a teenager and was now a grown woman. Eva also didn't like New York at first as it didn't meet the high expectations she had for the city. Mostly, however, Eva missed the Dutch foster family and Amsterdam, which she had come to love. In other respects, she enjoyed the hospitality of her family with her mother seeing some old friends in the city.

After a week's visit, Eva and her mother left New York and arrived in Michigan City, where her father greeted them with open arms at the railroad station during a heavy blizzard early in the morning. The entire family was reunited when Ruth came home from school for lunch. With the help of friends of the family, Eva soon found work with a company called Royal Metal, a manufacturer of metal furniture. Eva's job was to place a sticker on each piece of furniture as it came off the assembly line. Both the job and the limited social life in Michigan City left Eva bored and dissatisfied. She began to think about moving to New York.

In August 1947, the old Viennese family friends of the Broesslers, Endre and Jenny Sugar, who had left Austria and settled in Caracas, Venezuela, came to Michigan City for a visit. From there the Sugars planned to tour the United States, and they asked Eva to join them on their tour of the East Coast as her English was better than theirs. Eva jumped at the opportunity, and when they arrived in New York, she moved in with her relatives there, her Lampl uncles, aunts, and cousin Henry. She then secured temporary employment with a distant relative, a former Dutch attorney and diplomat, Eduard von Saher. He was the husband of Lilla Alexander van Saher, an author, former actress and one of Gustav's numerous Alexander cousins. Eva was hired to file von Saher's personal correspondence, a task she was well suited for as she now spoke and read Dutch, German and English.[23]

Once she had completed working for von Saher, Eva began to seek permanent employment and a place of her own. She found her way to the YMCA employment office and was referred to the Women's Hospital on Amsterdam Avenue, where she was hired as a clerk in the records department. She made very little money, but was able to afford the rent on a small room in the nurses' quarter of the hospital. Eva also enrolled in night courses in English and History with the intention of earning a high school diploma. She also completed a course in medical terminology.

Eva left New York for a time to return home in order to help care for Gustav, who had fallen seriously ill. After he recovered, Eva was invited to visit Caracas, Venezuela, for six months to see another part of the world and learn Spanish. She was the guest of the old family friends, the Sugars. There she became reacquainted with her childhood friend Ada, who was now married (to Arnold Rink) and had two children. She returned to the United States to keep her application for citizenship valid and to again be closer to her family. Eva now made her home permanently in the United States. She could, at last, begin to put the war behind her and begin life anew.

Eva's reunion with her family ended a long separation that she and her sister were fortunate to survive. Good fortune accompanied both girls from the time they left Vienna, through the war and occupation, until they rejoined their parents. The four Broesslers could not possibly have imagined that when the girls left Vienna that they would not gather again as a family until all of them had emigrated to the United States and eight years had passed. Nor could they have envisioned the events that would keep them apart for so long.

Much had been lost during those years of separation. The biggest loss, of course, was the opportunity for the Broesslers to live as a normal family in their native land. Instead, their lives were disrupted and they were forced by circumstances to leave their home in the hope that they could find a new start in the United States. None of them could have imagined the difficulties, challenges, obstacles and danger that they would have to survive and overcome in order to be reunited, or how long it would take. But they had endured and were finally together again, although the price they had paid was high. For Gustav and Thekla there were years of worry, doubt, fear and probably feelings of undue guilt that they had left their daughters behind in Nazi-occupied Europe. Could they have done more to get the girls out of Europe? Almost certainly both of them had to live with the helpless feeling that they could well have left Eva and Ruth behind to perish when they themselves came to America. Eva and Ruth found the separation from their parents equally difficult to bear. Despite the care and affection they received from their foster families, both girls missed their parents terribly. Living under conditions of extreme peril was difficult enough; to do so without one's family was even more so. Besides the care and affection Eva and Ruth received from their foster families, all they had to sustain them through these times was the hope that they would one day be reunited with their parents. Nor did they even have the solace of being together in these years. The girls lived with different families, and, while in the beginning they had visited each other as much as they could it was not the same as growing up together. And, once Eva went underground and Ruth and the Isaacs made their miraculous escape to Switzerland the sisters, though with wonderful people, were out of touch until war's end. Eva found herself alone, completely out of touch with her family, living as a hidden person with her life in danger every minute. Yet at the time of reunion in Michigan City, the separation from the foster family became painful too.

Lost also was the chance for their parents to see Eva and Ruth grow up. The two daughters who finally rejoined their parents were not the children who had boarded a train for The Netherlands on a cold January day in 1939. Ruth was a teenager when she was greeted joyfully by Gustav and Thekla in New York; Eva was a grown woman of twenty-three when she was reunited with her parents and sister. Those lost years could never be recaptured, and it is not surprising that Eva experienced feelings of ambivalence upon seeing her family again. It was she who had remained in The Netherlands through the duration of the war and she knew she was lucky to have survived. Although she never expressed it, if she felt some sense of anger or resentment that her parents and sister had escaped the Nazi regime while she had not, that would hardly be unusual.

The greatest loss of all was that of family and friends who had perished at the hands of the Nazis and their collaborators. The grief upon learning that so many had died was immense and it added to the struggle to adapt to the postwar world. Eva and the rest of her family would have to learn to cope with the fact that they had survived when so many had not.

Despite the losses, there were positives as well. Most importantly, the immediate family had survived. Despite the dangers, the hardships and the fear they had endured, they had all four found their way to the United States. Here they would put the past behind them and begin their lives anew in a land of possibilities and opportunity. Eva and Ruth would take advantage of these opportunities to move on to enjoy successful and productive lives.

Life in a new land did not mean that Eva and Ruth turned their backs on the old world. Survival came with the forging of lifelong connections to the European world they had left behind. Eva and Ruth each had second families—the Simons and Isaacs. They would remain in touch with their foster families throughout their lives, bound together by their common experiences and genuine affection for one another. In the same manner, lifelong friendships were formed with others who had survived or who helped others to escape the Nazi death machine. These connections undoubtedly helped Eva and Ruth cope with the feelings that arose as they dealt with the fact that they had survived the Holocaust when so many had not. Both women were able to move beyond their experiences in the Holocaust and become immersed in life once again.

Over time Eva and Ruth came to realize that, although neither of them had been in the death camps, their stories were equally important in the growing chronicles of the Holocaust. It is fortunate that they did, because their experiences offer a distinct perspective of the Holocaust. It is important to remember that some survivors escaped death by being hidden, or, in the case of Ruth and the Isaacs, by successfully escaping Nazi-occupied territory. Accounts such as these add to our understanding of the Holocaust and those who have lived to share their stories with the generations following. Eva and Ruth's survival is remarkable in many ways, especially in the great good fortune they experienced. Their survival is also a testament to the courage of those who helped them to live through these dangerous and terrifying times. In Eva's case, she truly was "hidden in plain sight." Eva was not concealed day and night in a room or closet or cellar, but lived relatively openly with only her false papers for dubious protection. It would have taken very little for her to have been arrested and transported to a concentration camp. A slip of the tongue, a simple betrayal by a neighbor, a more than cursory check of her false documents—any of these and more would have resulted in Eva's deportation and likely death. Without question, she was lucky, but she was also protected by courageous people who chose to defy the Nazis' Final Solution because, as a former member of the Dutch Resistance said, "It was the right thing to do." Thanks to the valor of the Simons and Isaac families, and others like them, many lived who would have otherwise perished.

NOTES

1. Broessler, *My Life*.
2. Weissman, "The War Came to Me."
3. Weissman, *Shoah*, Weissman, *Life*, Weissman, "The War Came to Me."
4. Ibid.; Broessler, *My Life*.
5. Broessler, *My Life*.

6. Ibid.
7. Ibid.
8. Ibid.
9. Ibid.
10. Ibid.
11. Ibid.
12. Ibid.
13. Ibid.
14. Ibid.
15. Ibid.
16. Ibid.
17. Weissman, "The War Came to Me."
18. Ibid.
19. Ibid.
20. Ibid.
21. Ibid.
22. Ibid.
23. Broessler, *My Life*.

Epilogue: A Life with a View

Indeed the war had come to me and to so many others. On May 5, 1945 the war was over, at least in The Netherlands where I had endured persecution and survived many narrow escapes. I was in Amsterdam and free of Nazi oppression when people enthusiastically welcomed the Canadian soldiers, our young liberators. From the day the war was over, my parents in the United States, my sister, then in Switzerland, and I worked on emigration and immigration to achieve the long-awaited family reunion in Michigan City, Indiana. My parents had lived there since 1940, proud new American citizens and members of a hospitable reformed Jewish community.

In the Netherlands, the war had come to me and the war was over. Wonderful as this was, it also represented a shock of different proportion, a mixture of joy and sadness, as well as anxiety about the pending separation from the Simons family, and anticipation of a new life in the United States, again in a new country. Joy about the war's end was coupled with sadness because millions of innocent people had perished. In my own immediate circle, my aunt Jetti (Henriette Broessler), my uncle Gustav Morton, my foster parents, Marinus and Caroline Simons; also relatives and friends who had been deported from Vienna, Budapest, Prague and other places as well as those of the Simons and Isaac families whom I considered my relatives by this time.

Heartbreaking and upsetting also were the stories of the survivors. My foster sisters Hannie and Tin Simons, who by an almost miracle had survived Auschwitz and other camps, returned through a rescue action via Sweden; in bad physical condition, with their concentration camp numbers tattooed on their arms. They and their sister Jobje, who had been a surviving "underduiker" in Amsterdam, had become orphans. They were plagued by their own tragedies as well as by the thoughts of the horrible death of their parents in the German camp Bergen-Belsen. Without parental guidance and support the girls had to start a new life in their war-torn homeland. The Simons family I had lived with in Utrecht—Oma and Tante Stel as I called them, had managed to survive the ghetto/camp Theresienstadt but Oma was deadly sick and did not live long after the tragedy. Tante Stel, strong as she was, energetically rebuilt her law practice at age 57 and lived to be 100, not unscarred, however, after the ordeals she had endured.

The reports of the Broessler family—Uncle Otto, Aunt Mitzi, and cousins Trude and Peter—told us how they had experienced extremely dangerous and difficult years as they survived in Vienna. How they had lived under truly traumatic circumstances, to say the least, would fill another book. It must be mentioned, however, that notwithstanding their hardships and their own lack of sufficient food, they even shared their meager rations and sent small care packages to Theresienstadt when that was still possible. Nobody knows whether these treasured gifts were always distributed. Yet these selfless presents were sent to their incarcerated friends, including Oma and Tante Stel because they had been so good to me. These blood relatives and foster relatives never met but even after the war they corresponded with each other in German and addressed each other sentimentally as "Onkel Otto und Tante Stel."

My other relatives, the Lampl family, had in spite of many hurdles, been able to settle in New York but they too were not free of anguish and anxiety. Aside from the difficulties of obtaining work as new immigrants, they were in constant worry about their parents who were stuck in Austria. Uncle Max, aunt Pauline and son Henry (formerly Heinz), relieved that the war had ended, received the devastating news that my aunt's parents had committed suicide. Uncle Felix and Aunt Hilda after many worries finally learned that my aunt's parents had miraculously survived a very bad part of the Theresienstadt ghetto; finally they did come to the United States, old and broken. The Weissenberg girls I mentioned in my prologue were separated from each other for years; their father and mother were each in different countries. They too learned that Omama (Grandmother) Weissenberg had killed herself in Vienna when she was supposed to be deported. Such was life when the war had ended and joy was coupled with sadness.

As reported in the previous chapter of this book, 1945 passed, Spring 1946 started and what sticks most in my mind are the constant attempts at emigration and their bureaucratic hurdles. Finally, my sister was able to leave Switzerland in May and after three weeks with my foster family and me in Amsterdam, she first saw the Statue of Liberty in New York in June of 1946. I was not able to do so until the end of January 1947, when life in the new world started for me.

I came to the United States without financial means, no profession, and no trade, forced to earn a living without the necessary formal education to pursue a college degree. It was to my advantage that in the America of the 1950s and 1960s, there were still job opportunities available to individuals who were willing to work hard and were ready to learn on the job. With perseverance, understanding parents and new friends, plus good luck, I worked myself up from a clerk in the record room of a hospital, to a field director for the National Council of Jewish Women, to Executive Director of the Myasthenia Gravis Foundation. I eventually worked as the head of Foundation Relations for Case Western Reserve University in Cleveland, Ohio. My experiences during the war have uniquely suited me to work in the nonprofit sector, as they have taught me the importance of compassion and of service to others.

These values were constantly reinforced to me through the example of my parents. They had made such a great adjustment from their life in Europe to their new life in America, without expressing any resentment toward their change in circumstances. They had earned the respect of the community in Michigan City, as they had before in Vienna and are remembered for their integrity, humanity and hospitality. They had made a home for Ruth and me and also for our cousins Trude and Peter Broessler when they came to the United States in 1949 and 1951 respectively.

A year after my father's death on January 5, 1958, I had a very small wedding in my mother's home in Michigan City, Indiana, on April 19, 1959. Oscar Weissman and I had met in Chicago at Michael Reese Hospital and Medical Center where he was Medical Director and I the Executive Secretary of the Medical Staff. Oscar was divorced and had two teenage children, Andy and Judy, who readily befriended me. They easily accepted their visits and periodic stays in the home their father and I built. Oscar was a physician who after studies at Columbia University received his medical degree from Long Island College of Medicine in New York. In addition, he had a Master's Degree in Public Health from Harvard University. A hospital administrator, educator and public health director, he was a pioneer in health reform and an advocate for good health care for all.

All of us in the family and many of the guests who visited us still remember Oscar's vast collection of books, including his fine professional library. Oscar was extremely well read and had an uncanny ability to come up with particularly pertinent reference sources for the most esoteric subject under discussion.

We always lived in high-rise buildings: first in Chicago, then from 1961 through 1965 in Pittsburgh, followed by Manhattan from 1966 until 1973 when we moved from New York to metropolitan Cleveland—to Lakewood to be exact. In all these places we enjoyed our lovingly lived-in apartments that overlooked Lake Michigan in Chicago, the Monongahela River in Pittsburgh, the skyscrapers of Manhattan in New York and Lake Erie in Cleveland. Our living quarters gave us joy. We gladly shared this joy with others who too found pleasure in sharing good meals and good conversation while enjoying with us the panoramic view from on high.

Perhaps it was our joy in creating a comfortable home, our shared taste and style, and our open-door policy that kept us together so happily. Although our personalities were different—Oscar was introspective and quiet, while I am outgoing—we shared the same worldview and a common sense of humor. We each had interesting work that brought us together with like-minded people from all realms of life, as well as people of rather different backgrounds and sometimes opposing opinions.

In these early years of our marriage—though missing my father—at last my mother too found some, albeit short, happiness. She enjoyed frequent visits and seeing her two daughters and niece Trude with good husbands, becoming grandmother of Katya (Ruth's daughter) and great-aunt to Danny (Daniel Otto) and Linda Henriette Lasner (Trude's children). (Trude had selected the middle names of her children in memory of her father, Otto Broessler, and of our aunt, Dr. Henriette Broessler, "Aunt Jetti," who had died in an unknown concentration camp.) She was also happy to be a witness at the wedding of our cousin, Peter Broessler. Mama had proudly become the matriarch of the remaining members of the Broessler and Lampl clan. Only 65 years old, she died on April 7, 1963. As was the case when Papa had died, a large crowd of mourners paid their last respects. The few pieces of china, table linens, and mementos that had survived the Holocaust had graced the Broessler home in Michigan City. These now have tremendous sentimental and symbolic value for the family. Michigan City still is my sister's and my original American hometown.

While Oscar and I were busy creating our new life, in Chicago, Pittsburgh and New York, we were keenly aware of the events of the times, and emotionally involved in the Civil Rights Movement, the Feminist Movement and the Vietnam War. At the same time, we felt that not only political upheavals but also new technology were starting to shape and change our society. Unfortunately, our 28 years of marriage passed by much too quickly. Oscar died of lung cancer in our home in Lakewood, Ohio on February 13, 1987. His urn was interred in my parents' grave in Michigan City. More and more do I feel now how Oscar had strongly and very positively influenced my life while generously allowing me to develop my character in my own way and at my own pace.

Having been widowed for many years, I continue as best as possible to appreciate what life has to offer. I am active in community service, for many years as president of the Lakewood Public Library Foundation and in various key positions for the Huntington's Disease Society of America (HDSA). No work history would be complete without mentioning at least briefly my ongoing HDSA volunteer work to further this national organization's support of research, family care and education of the professional and general public. Sometimes Huntington's Disease is called "Woody Guthrie's Disease" because the famous folksinger by that name had died of the illness. His widow, the late Marjorie Guthrie, almost single handedly started a national and soon international movement to combat Huntington's Disease. She became a role model to many and inspired me too to work with zest and zeal as a part of the volunteer leadership. Dr. Alan Tartakoff referred to these endeavors in the foreword of this book.

In April of 2008, during a short visit to Austria, my sister and I received a cordial welcome by the current owner of our ancestral home and an equally friendly reception by the mayor and also the director of the city museum of Bad Vöslau. We realized that a new and kinder generation is now in charge. Similarly, the director and faculty of my high school in Vienna—which I had been forced to leave in 1938 only because I was a Jew—they too exemplify a return to democracy in Austria.

I continue to keep in touch with relatives and friends, by telephone and email and also by periodic visits to them in the United States, Canada and Europe. Oscar's children—Andy and Judy, and their children, Dana, Joshua and Tanya—and now their families keep me connected with the new generations. For the young ones I have become their "Oma." The bond with my sister and her family has become particularly strong even though our World War II experiences were different and even though we live 2,000 miles apart—she is in California, I am in Ohio. Ruth, her husband Leonard Newmark, and their children, Katya, her husband, Matthew Costello, and Mark, have always opened their home to me most lovingly. My nephew Mark wrote about me: "Was there ever a parent's sibling who was so approachable to her sibling's kids as our aunt Eva?" His sister, my niece, Katya, was the one who, as a little girl, asked whether I had to go to the war. Smiling at her innocent question, I answered: "No my dear, the war came to me," realizing that she did not yet understand what the war really was.

Years later, Katya described and illustrated my story as "a life with a view," partly because of our home in high-rise dwellings, but mainly because of my life's experiences. A loving family, selfless friends, a happy marriage, my interesting jobs and volunteer positions, not to mention healthy genes and good luck, they all provided learning experiences and joy—truly a life with a view!

Eva Broessler Weissman
July 2008
Lakewood, Ohio

Appendix

INFORMAL GUIDE TO THE BROESSLER FAMILY

Parents of Sigmund Broessler:
Pinkus Broessler (1820–1891), brother of Juda Broessler—Fanni Grün (1834–1907)

Parents of Betti (Berta) Broessler:
Juda Broessler (1818–1907), brother of Pinkus Broessler—Hanna Grünwald (1834–1907)

Sigmund Broessler (1858–1919)—Betti (Berta) Broessler (1859–1929)
1. Henriette Ida (Jetti) Broessler (1889—unknown, died in concentration camp)
2. Gustav (Gustl) Broessler (1891–1958)—Thekla Lampl (1897–1962)
   Eva Gertrud Broessler Weissman (1923–)—Oscar Israel Weissman (1908–1987)
   Ruth Sylvia Broessler Newmark (1931–)—Leonard Daniel Newmark (1929–)
3. Margarete (Grete) Broessler (1895–1942)—Gustav Morton (1889—unknown, died in concentration camp)
4. Otto Wolfgang Broessler (1898–1952)—Maria (Mitzi) Kornherr (1896–1983)
   Gertrude Maria (Trude/Trudy) Broessler Lasner (1928–)—Fred (Fritz) Lasner (1911–1980)
   Peter Heinz Broessler (1932–)—Joan (nee Blade) (1931–)

Note on the Broessler Family: Broessler descendents born after World War II include Ruth's children Katya Lisa (born 1959) and Mark Sigurd (born 1967). Katya is married to G. Matthew Costello, and they have two children, Danya Lena and Justin Alexander. Other Broessler descendents include Trude and Fred Lasner's children: their son Daniel Otto (born 1952) and daughter Linda Henriette (born 1955). Daniel is married to Allison (nee Margolis) and has a son, Joel. Linda is married to Bradley Berkowitz and has two children, Sam and Marni.

There are many first, second and third cousins with whom Eva and Ruth remain in touch. These include Judith Laqueur, the daughter of Géza and Magda Révész, her son Matthias and family, and her daughter Madeleine; Judith's first cousins, Catherine, Vera, and Robin Alexander; Stella Moore and, of an even younger generation, Szusi Rényi. Even though these relatives live in various parts of the United States and Europe, there is a strong bond among the members of the original Broessler clan. The last Broessler descendant still living in Vienna is Ronald Barazon, a third cousin, who has inherited a terrific sense of humor plus many true and fictitious Broessler family stories that still need recording. Gerald (Gerry) Golden keeps a Broessler family tree. His mother was a born Broessler but the exact relationship has yet to be figured out. It is known only that in the nineteenth century, during the Austro-Hungarian monarchy, most of the Broesslers lived in Ungarisch Brod (Moravia) while others have claimed that the original Broesslers were Sephardic Jews who came from Brussels.

INFORMAL GUIDE TO THE LAMPL FAMILY

Parents of Salomon Lampl:
Moses (Moische) Lampl — Johanna (Hanni) (Maiden name unknown)

Parents of Paula Pollaczek:
Maximilian Pollaczek (1826–1882) — Julie Brentano (1842–1925)

Salomon (Sigmund) Lampl (1863–1937) — Paula Pollaczek (1867–1933)
  1. Thekla Lampl Broessler (1897–1962) — Gustav (Gustl) Broessler (1891–1958)
     Eva Gertrud Broessler Weissman (1923–)
     Ruth Sylvia Broessler Newmark (1931–)
  2. Maximilian (Max) Lampl (1899–1982) — Pauline (Pauli) Placzek (1904–1989)
     Heinz (Henry) Lampl (1928–1996)
  3. Felix Lampl (1900–1970) — Hildegard (Hilda) Wolf (1906–1989)

Note on the Lampl Family: Eva and Ruth's mother Thekla was born a Lampl, whose family chronology is not well known. An elaborate family tree including Thekla's mother, Paula Pollaczek, and her ancestors does exist and includes Brentano and other notable names.

INFORMAL GUIDE TO THE SIMONS FAMILY

David Simons (1860–1930)—Marianne Simons-van Raalte ("Oma") (1863–1947)
  1. Estella C. Simons ("Tante Stel") (1888–1989)
  2. Marinus Simons (1891–1945)—Caroline Simons-Edersheim (1896–1945)
    Sophie Marianne van den Bergh-Simons ("Jobje") (1922–)
    Hannie Ligtenstein-Simons (1925–1989)
    Judith Gompen-Simons ("Tin") (1927–)

Note: Eva has kept in touch with Jobje, Hannie, and Tin, and their families, throughout the years.

Philip Simons (1868–1940)—Johanna Simons-van Hamersveld ("Mommy") (1884–1956)
  1. Erika Grace Line Simons ("Eka," in Canada called "Katy") (1911–2005)
  2. Siebert Philip Simons (1922–2007)
    Renée Philipine (1956–)
    Ruth Margaret Simons (1958–)
  3. Euphemia Henriette Maria Simons ("Phemia") (1924–)

Note: Because of her contacts with the Simons family in the United States, Eva's connection with the Simons family has continued to grow. Siebert Simons' daughter Ruth, husband Paul Gossen, and children Frances and Alex live in Louisville, Kentucky and visit Eva regularly, as do Roby Simons of Cleveland and his family. Roby (Robert Allen) is a distant Simons cousin but he and his family (including four Simons sons) are good friends of the Louisville relatives. They all consider Eva their "Tante" (aunt).

INFORMAL GUIDE TO THE ISAAC FAMILY

Arthur Aaron Isaac (1858–1932)—Ella Isaac Goudsmit (1866–1955)
  1. Siegfried Isaac ("Frits") (1900–1948)—Elisa Hermine Isaac-Edersheim ("Elly") (1903–1999)

Henriette de Levita-Isaac ("Jet") (1929–)
Arthur Daniel Isaac (1932–)
Benjamin Henri Isaac (1945–)

Note: Jet, Arthur, and Ben are Ruth's foster siblings and Ruth and her family maintain close relationships with them and their families.

Note on names: In The Netherlands the custom is for the surnames of married women to list the married name first, hyphenated with the maiden name. For Eva and Ruth's names, standard American practice is used.

EVA G. WEISSMAN
EMPLOYMENT AND VOLUNTEER HISTORY

Organizational Development, Grants Management, and Fundraising, specializing in the nonprofit field; Certified Fundraising Executive

Employment

Cleveland: Case Western Reserve University: Director of Foundation Relations with special assignment to the School of Medicine and the Mandel School for Applied Social Sciences

University Hospitals of Cleveland: Consultant to Development Department

New York City: Myasthenia Gravis Foundation: National Executive Director; represented Foundation on U.S. President's Committee on Employment of the Handicapped

National Council of Jewish Women: National Field Director, responsible for chapter program planning, fundraising, and legislative advocacy

Pittsburgh: University of Pittsburgh School of Medicine: Child Development Department; Coordinator and Assistant to Chairman

Chicago: Michael Reese Hospital Medical Center: Registrar, Postgraduate School; Assistant to Director of Research Institute; Manager, Office of Medical Staff and Alumni Association

Commission on Chronic Illness: (co-sponsored by the American Medical Association and the U.S. Public Health Service); Office Manager of multi-year research study

Major Volunteer Positions

Huntington's Disease Society of America:

National: National Trustee on Executive Committee; Chairperson of Leadership Committee; Chairperson of

National Convention; Member National Marketing Committee; Received two of the highest achievement awards; Board Representative at International Huntington Association meetings in Italy, Canada, and Belgium

Northeast Ohio Chapter: Chapter Charter Member; served two three-year terms as Chapter President; Life Director; Chairperson of Nominations and Governance Committee

Winton Place, 350 Unit Condominium Association:
Served two three-year terms on Board of Managers

Lakewood Public Library:
Served ten years, as Vice President and President of the Lakewood Public Library Foundation

July 2008

LETTER WRITTEN BY EVA WEISSMAN TO YAD VASHEM IN JERUSALEM ON BEHALF OF ERIKA G.L. SIMONS AUGUST 31, 1999

To Whom It May Concern:

Through her humanitarian efforts Miss Erika G.L. Simons (called Eka by her friends and relatives), born on February 13, 1911, saved my life and that of many other Jews and Dutch citizens at risk. Numerous friends and Jewish colleagues at a University of Amsterdam laboratory depended on her for bringing food to hiding places, storing their belongings, and engaging the participation of her younger brother and sister. However, this report is confined to my own experiences, in gratitude for her and her family's kindness to me.

Born in Vienna, I came to Holland in January of 1939 to escape Nazi persecution in Austria. I met Eka shortly thereafter and became the beneficiary of her compassionate initiatives during the Nazi occupation of the Netherlands. Specifically, after I was miraculously released from the *Amsterdam Strafgevangenis* in August 1942, Eka and her equally compassionate mother allowed me to find shelter in their home: P.C. Hooftstraat 41, in Amsterdam. This was done at risk to the entire family, which included Mrs. Johanna Simons-van Hamersveld, Eka, her brother Siebert P. Simons, and her younger sister, Euphemia H.M. Simons. They provided not only shelter—under very trying circumstances—but also food, since as a refugee I had no money at all and no other access to food.

My stay in the P.C. Hooftstraat was originally intended to last but a few weeks, but circumstances dictated that I was to remain in hiding there until the end of the war, and in many ways to become a member of the family until my emigration to the United States in January of 1947. During the war and especially during the last *hongerwinter*, the Simons home became a haven not only for me but also for three, four, and at one time even six, other *onderduikers*. In those years, Eka managed to obtain a false identity card for me under the name of Johanna Cornelia Meijer, as well as periodically some illegally-obtained food coupons. Together with the family's own small ration allotments, this gave us scarcely enough for the essentials we all needed to survive.

Eka's mother, Mamie (Johanna Simons-van Hamersveld), worthy of posthumous recognition in her own right, was the widowed owner of a stationery store, but had little merchandise to sell. Nevertheless, people wandered into the store, so that having *onderduikers* upstairs was extremely dangerous. Mamie was called to the Gestapo several times, but somehow, she managed to continue her good work steadfastly, saving the lives of innocent people, in spite of the danger.

Eka Simons herself spent many weeks in jail after having been arrested when found trying to rescue Jews. At further risk to herself, she did courier work for the Dutch underground, especially during the harsh winter of 1944–45. Undernourished and in poor physical condition, she herself was taken in by good people in Groningen, while in Amsterdam her mother continued to look after me, Karel Levisson, Sophie M. Simons, and frequent short-term *onderduikers*.

After the war, neighbors and other store owners in the P.C. Hooftstraat revealed that most of them knew of the rescue efforts of the Simons family members. That they did not report them to the German authorities evidenced their own moral stance as well as their respect for the Simons family.

While no official recognition could suffice as recompense for all that the whole Simons family did to save my life, I recommend that Eka Simons be singled out and honored now for her especially courageous behavior in dangerous days.

Eva G. Weissman

Both Eka (in Canada called Katy) Simons and her mother each received this prestigious award. Eva attended the awards ceremony for Johanna Simons in Amsterdam and for Eka Simons in Winnipeg, Canada with Eka's niece Ruth Simons and Ruth's daughter Frances.

REFLECTION
AUCH ICH WAR EINST EIN WIENERKIND
(I TOO WAS ONCE VIENNA'S CHILD) ODE
TO THE BILLROTHGYMNASIUM

It was a great pleasure to be invited by Frau Direktor Mag. Ursula Madl and Prof. Horst Prentler to address students of the Billrothgymnasium on April 7 and 8, 2008, during my recent visit to Vienna. It was a special honor that other teachers, as well as Mrs. Ellen Stern, Director of the American International School, Vienna and Bezirksvorsteher Adolf Tiller, were also in attendance. I treasure the book "Doebling" by Godehard Schwarz, generously given to me by Mr. Tiller with inscription. It provides an inspiring memento that prompts me to reflect on my school years in Doebling from 1933 to 1938. I have tried to describe these years in person in April of this year, but now, a few months later, I feel that additional words in writing may be in order.

Having lived in Waehring on the periphery of Doebling and attended the Volksschule in the Koehlergasse, I entered in September of 1933 the Doeblinger Maedchen Mittelschule (later Realgymnasium, presently Billrothgymnasium). An entrance exam was required and I had proudly passed it. I was a Wienerkind of a comfortable middle class family, expected to grow up with a solid, basic basic education. Attendance of four years Volksschule and eight years Realgymnasium had been planned, ultimately to be capped by the successful completion of the Matura. Such eight years of schooling in a Gymnasium would be considered an equivalent of high school plus two years of college in the United States. Unfortunately, world events prevented me from obtaining a diploma, this coveted achievement award. Not having this degree has bothered me, perhaps unduly, for most of my life. I even developed a certain feeling of intellectual inferiority, especially vis-à-vis my late husband, Dr. Oscar Weissman, and certain members of my family and friends, all with even much higher academic degrees than a Matura. This feeling of inferiority, however, was counterbalanced by my strong desire to belong to, and my ready ability to fit into, well-educated circles. After having taken a few special courses and having done well in my jobs, I slowly overcame my feelings of inadequacy. Vaguely, I remember having seen a plaque somewhere that stated: *Not for school, but for life we learn*. How true this was for me!

Of course, I cannot forget that in 1938, after a total of only nine years of schooling, I was forced to interrupt my formal education simply because I was a Jew. Though fortunate to be able to emigrate to the Netherlands, in 1940 Hitler invaded that country too. Again I was persecuted, separated for eight years from my parents and only sister, not to speak of the loss of family and friends who perished in concentration camps. Under trying circumstances, to say the least, I survived the Holocaust in the Netherlands.

I came to the United States in 1947 without financial means, no profession, no trade, forced to earn a living, once more in a new country with a different language and a different way of life. As different as this language was from German and Dutch—which I spoke fluently—I had learned English from an early age on, and already had a pretty good command of grammar and spelling. I quickly switched from the British English I had learned to the American English spoken. Notwithstanding that I have maintained the ability to speak and write German, I write these thoughts in English, as this may reflect my current way of expression more vividly.

I feel keenly that my parental home and surroundings, my early school years, and my life with many caring people who risked their lives to shelter me, have enabled me to cope with life's adversities. In the years that followed, I managed to augment my meager but still fundamental school knowledge. I regret that I missed many opportunities for book learning, but does anybody ever take advantage of all available resources? After all, we do not learn for school but life.

I attended a girls' school where we, at least I, showed little interest in science. This has changed, but clearly the spirit of a well run co-educational institution with emphasis on the humanities prevails at the Billrothgymnasium. How else would it have been possible for students and teachers to come, listen to my life's story, and to ask pertinent questions?

To all who have greeted me so kindly, my sincere thanks, especially to Director Madl and her administrative and teaching staff for the warm welcome, and, in words that I find difficult to express, my heartfelt appreciation to Professor Horst Prentler for so empathetically ensuring that the horrors of the Holocaust be not forgotten.

As a Wienerkind with roots now firmly planted in the Unites States, I gladly acknowledge the good I have experienced in my childhood: in my parental home, in the homes of my Dutch foster family, and in the Billrothgymnasium—it all lasted me a lifetime.

I am honored that this letter was subsequently published in the school's 2007/2008 Yearbook and that I was made an honorary member of the Society of the Friends of the Billrothgymnasium.

Eva G. Weissman
June 2008

Selected Bibliography

PRIMARY SOURCES

Broessler, Ruth. *My Life*. Unpublished memoir.
Correspondence between Eva Broessler Weissman and Gregory Moore, August 25, 2005.
Newmark, Ruth. *Shoah*. USC Shoah Foundation Institute for Visual History and Education. Copy of the videotape on file in the Tolerance Resource Center, Notre Dame College, South Euclid, Ohio.
Newmark, Ruth. Unpublished memoir. 2006.
"On the Establishment of Jewish Labor Camps in the Netherlands, January 1942." *Het Joodsche Weekblad*, January 9, 1942. Shoah Resource Center, The International School for Holocaust Studies. www.yadvashem.org.
Oral interviews between Eva Broessler Weissman and Gregory Moore, 2005–2007.
Weissman, Eva G. *A Life with a View*. Unpublished memoir.
Weissman, Eva G. *Shoah*. USC Shoah Foundation Institute for Visual History and Education. Copy of the videotape on file in the Tolerance Resource Center, Notre Dame College, South Euclid, Ohio.

SECONDARY SOURCES

Ajzensztadt, Amnon. *Endurance: Chronicles of Jewish Resistance*. Ontario: Mosaic Press, 1987.
Bauer, Yehuda. *A History of the Holocaust*. New York: Franklin Watts, 1982.
Beller, Steven. *A Concise History of Austria*. Cambridge: Cambridge University Press, 2006.
Berenbaum, Michael, ed. *Witness to the Holocaust*. New York: Harper Collins, 1997.
Berenbaum, Michael, ed. *The World Must Know*. New York: Little, Brown & Co., 1993.

Breitman, Richard. *The Architect of Genocide*. New York: Knopf, 1991.
Cargas, Harry James, ed. *When God and Man Failed: Non-Jewish Views of the Holocaust*. New York: Macmillan, 1981.
Cohen, Arthur A., ed. *Arguments and Doctrines: A Reader of Jewish Thinking in the Aftermath of the Holocaust*. New York: Harper & Row, 1970.
Dawidowicz, Lucy S. *The War Against the Jews, 1939–1945*. New York: Holt, Rinehart and Winston, 1975.
Dawidowicz, Lucy S. *A Holocaust Reader*. New York: Behrman House, 1976.
Edelheit, Abraham & Herschel. *History of the Holocaust: A Handbook and Dictionary*. Boulder, (CO): Westview Press, 1994.
Edersheim, Maurits E. *A Life Without Borders: A Memoir*. 2000.
Fogelman, Eva. *Conscience and Courage: Rescuers of Jews During the Holocaust*. New York: Doubleday, 1994.
Friedlander, Henry. *The Origins of Nazi Genocide: From Euthanasia to the Final Solution*. Chapel Hill: The University of North Carolina Press, 1995.
Friedländer, Saul. *Nazi Germany and the Jews, Volume I: The Years of Persecution, 1933–1939*. New York: Harper Collins, 1997.
Friedländer, Saul. *Nazi Germany and the Jews, Volume II; The Years of Extermination, 1939–1945*. New York, Harper Collins, 2007.
Friedman, Arnold. *Death Was Our Destiny*. New York: Vantage Press, 1972.
Gilbert, Martin. *The Holocaust: A History of the Jews During the Second World War*. New York: Henry Holt, 1985.
Gutman, Israel, ed. *Encyclopedia of the Holocaust*. New York: Macmillan, 1990.
Harran, Marilyn, Dieter Kuntz, et.al. *The Holocaust Chronicle*. Lakewood, Illinois: Publications International, Ltd., 2003.
Hatzair, Hashomer. *The Massacre of European Jewry: An Anthology*. Israel, 1963.
Hilberg, Raul. *The Destruction of the European Jews*. New York: Holmes & Meier, 1985.
Hilberg, Raul. *Perpetrators, Victims, Bystanders: The Jewish Catastrophe, 1933–1945*. New York: Harper Collins, 1992.
Hillesum, Etty. *An Interrupted Life: The Diaries of Etty Hillesum, 1941–1943*. New York: Pantheon, 1983.
Hillesum, Etty. *Letters from Westerbork*. New York: Pantheon, 1986.
Hilsenrad, Helen. *Brown was the Danube: A Memoir of Hitler's Vienna*. New York: Thomas Yoseloff, 1966.
Holliday, Laurel, ed. *Children in the Holocaust and World War II*. New York: Washington Square Press, 1995.
Johnston, William M. *The Austrian Mind: An Intellectual and Social History, 1848–1938*. Berkeley: University of California Press, 1972.
Landau, Ronnie S. *The Nazi Holocaust*. Chicago: Ivan R. Dee, 1994.
Littman, L.T.S. *Ashley Chase: A Dorset Domain*. Gloucester: Alan Sutton Publishing, 1988.
Michael, Robert A. *The Holocaust: A Chronicle and Documentary*. Northvale (NJ): Jason Aronson, 1998.

Michel, Henri. *The Shadow War: European Resistance, 1939–1945.* New York: Harper & Row, 1942.

Pelser, Henk E. *Henk's War: A Memoir of the Dutch Underground.* London: Portell Productions, 2006.

Polak, Jaap, and Ina Soep. *Steal a Pencil for Me: Love Letters from Camp Bergen-Belsen Westerbork.* Scarsdale: Lion, 2000.

Presser, Jacob. *Ashes in the Wind: The Destruction of Dutch Jewry.* Detroit: Wayne State University Press, 1998.

Pulzer, Peter G. J. *The Rise of Political Anti-Semitism in Germany and Austria.* New York: John Wiley & Sons, 1964.

Rossel, Seymour. *The Holocaust: The World and the Jews, 1933–1945.* West Orange (NJ): Behrman House, 1992.

Schloss, Eva, and Barbara Powers. *The Promise.* London: Penguin, 2006.

Silver, Eric. *The Book of the Just: The Unsung Heroes Who Rescued Jews from Hitler.* New York: Grove Press, 1992.

Stone, Kay. *Katy Simons: A Memoir and a Tribute.* Unpublished memoir, 2003.

Teitelbaum, Freda Ulman. *Vienna Revisited.* Santa Barbara: Fithian, 1995.

Warmbrunn, Werner. *The Dutch Under German Occupation, 1940–1945.* Stanford: Stanford University Press, 1963.

Wasserstein, Bernard. *Britain and the Jews of Europe, 1939–1945.* New York: Oxford University Press, 1979.

Zelman, Leon, and Armin Thurnher, trans. Meredith Schneeweiss. *After Survival: One Man's Mission in the Cause of Memory.* New York: Holmes & Meier, 1998.

Index

Achatz, Rosi, 9
Action groups. *See Knokploegen*
Alexander, Franz, 19
Allies, 61
America. *See* United States
American Consulate, 66
Amsterdam, The Netherlands, 22, 29–30, 35, 37–40, 45, 54, 61, 66–67, 70–71, 77
Amsterdam Jews, 32
Anschluss, 5–17
Anti-Semites, 55
Anti-Semitism, 7, 9–10, 15, 17, 18, 54
Antwerp, Belgium, 46
A. Puls Company, 55
Ardennes Forest, 47
Aryan, 17
Aryanized, 17
Ashley Chase, 24–25, 29
Asscher, Abraham, 33
Atlantic Ocean, 67
Auschwitz, 39, 62
Austria, xv, xvii, 1–2, 10, 14, 17–18, 20, 68, 81
Austrian Jews, 1, 12, 14, 16
Austrian Nazis, 9–10, 14
Austro-Hungarian Empire, 2
Authoritarianism, 1

Bad Vöslau, 4, 9, 16, 81
Bauer, Otto, 3
Belgium, 46, 70
Bergen-Belsen, 62, 77
Bettelheim, Bruno, 21
Bijenkorf, 20, 45
Black Market, 69
Bodegraven, 30
Bouillon, Belgium, 47
Brenner Pass, 11
British Broadcasting Corporation (BBC), 58–59, 61
Broessler, Betti (Berta), 9
Broessler, Eva Gertrud, 1–2, 5–6, 14–16, 18–20, 2 1–25, 30–31, 33–35, 37–40, 43, 45, 48, 53–62, 64–74, 77–81
Broessler Family, 1, 5, 62, 80
Broessler, Gustav, ix, 1, 4, 9, 18, 20, 23–26, 29, 31, 35, 64–69, 72–73, 78–79
Broessler, Henriette (Jetti), 9, 77, 80
Broessler, Maria (Mitzi), 18, 62, 78
Broessler, Margarete (Grete), 9
Broessler, Otto, 9, 62, 69, 78, 80
Broessler, Peter Heinz, 62, 78–80
Broessler, Ruth Sylvia, ix, 1–2, 9, 18, 20, 23–25, 30–31, 33–35, 43–52, 55–56, 60, 64–68, 71, 73–74, 79, 81

Broessler, Sigmund, 1, 9
Broessler, Thekla, ix, 1–2, 9, 18, 20, 23–26, 29, 31, 35, 64–69, 71–73, 79–80
Broessler, Gertrude Maria (Trude/Trudy), 62, 78–80
Brussels, Belgium, 44, 46–48, 70
Budapest, Hungary, 62, 77

Camp Büren, 51
Caracas, Venezuela, 71–72
Casablanca, 70
Catholicism, 8
Central Agency for Jewish Emigration (*Zentralstelle für Jüdische Auswanderung*), 33–34, 36
Central Office for Jewish Emigration (*Zentralstelle für Jüdische Auswanderung*), 18
Chaplin, Charlie, xv
Chicago, Illinois, 79–80
China, 18
Christian Democrats, 2, 4
Christian Socialist Party, 2, 11
Christian Socialists, 11
Cigarettes, 69–70
Clarens, Switzerland, 51
Cleveland, Ohio, 79
Cohen, David, 33
Cologne, Germany, 21, 48
Columbia University, 79
Communist Party (Communism/Communists), 3, 16
Concentration camp, 16, 61–62, 74
Concertgebouw, 70
Costello, Matthew, 81
Cuba, 18
Czechoslovakia, 2

Dachau, 16–17
Death camps, 35, 38–39, 50, 67
de Boer, Sylvia (Ruth Broessler), 46
de Laet, Sylvia (Ruth Broessler), 46
de Jong, Dick, 45

Denmark, 26
Deutsch, Julius, 3
Dictatorship, 11
Disponent, 1
Dollfuss, Englebert, 10–11
Dutch Censorship Office, 69
Dutch Jews, 29, 32, 36, 43, 54, 57
Dutch National Socialist Movement (NSB), 28
Dutch Resistance, 29, 36–37, 39–40, 44–45, 54–55, 60, 74
Dutch Supreme Court, 33

Ecole Internationale, 52
Edersheim, Henri, 43
Edersheim, Karel, 38
Eichmann, Adolf, 16
Eighteenth District (Vienna), 5, 8
Enemy aliens, 29
Engl, Hansi (Kennedy), 5
Euterpestraat, 38
Exemption stamps. See Sperrsstempel

Fascism, xvi
Fatherland Front, 11
Final Solution, 15, 74
Fischer, Franz, 43
France, 47, 50
Freiwilligen Legion Niederlander (Dutch Volunteer Legion), 55
French Resistance, 48–49
Freud, Anna, 5

Gates of Nancy (France), 48
Geb. Hirsch & Cie., 69
Geneva, Switzerland, 52
Gentiles, 14, 54
German Jews, 10
Germany, 17, 28
Gersthoferstrasse, 8, 16
Gestapo, 35–40, 59–60
Gone With the Wind, 70
Great Britain, 21, 24
Great Depression, 8–9

Guthrie, Marjorie, 81
Guthrie, Woody, 81
Gymnasium, 5

Hague, The, 23, 30, 35, 38, 43, 45, 65, 70
Hakenkreuzler (Swastika Men), 4, 9
Handelsakademie, 1
Harding, Warren G., xv
Harvard University, 79
Hebrew, 22
Heijplaat, 22
Heimwehr (Home Defense), 3
Heinrich Klinger, 1, 17
Hempstead Child Therapy Clinic, 5
Hérimoncourt, France, 49–50
Het Parool (*The Parole*), 59–60, 69
Hilsenrad, Helen, 15
Hitler, Adolf, 1, 10, 14
Holland. *See* Netherlands, The, 25, 65
Holocaust, 1, 5, 74
Hotel Beau-Site, 51
Hotel Jeanne d'Arc, 47
Hungary, 2, 62
Huntington's Disease Society of America (HDSA), 80–81

Ijmuiden, 30
Indianapolis, Indiana, 31
Innitzer, Theodor (Cardinal), 15
Ireland, 67, 71
Isaac, Arthur, 23
Isaac, Benjamin, 23, 52
Isaac, Elly, 23, 33, 43, 47, 49–52
Isaac Family, 20, 22–23, 31, 35, 62, 67. 72, 74
Isaac, (Siegfried) Frits, 23, 33, 43–45, 47, 49–52, 65–67
Isaac, Jet, 23, 48
Isle of Man, 29
Israelitsche Kultusgemeinde, 5, 17
Italy, 11

Jewish Coordinating Committee (*Joodsche Coördinatie Commissie*), 32

Jewish Council (*Joodsche Raad*), 32–33, 38–39, 43, 55
Jewish Refugee Committee, 66
Joodsche Weekblad, 36
Judenrat, 32
Jura Mountains, 49, 51

Kemenyi, Anna, 17
Ketjen (chemical manufacturing company), 45
Kindertransport, 21
Klosters, Switzerland, 65
Knokploegen (action groups), 32
Kray, Ivonne (Sokolow), 71
Kristallnacht, 18
Kronberger, Elsa, 29

Labor camps, 43
Lake Erie, 79
Lake Geneva, 51
Lake Michigan, 68, 79
Lakewood, Ohio, 79–80
Lakewood Public Library Foundation, 80
Lampl, Felix, 31, 78
Lampl, Heinz (Henry), 71, 78
Lampl, Hildegard (Hilda), 9, 31, 78
Lampl, Maximilian (Max), 9, 31, 78
Lampl, Pauline (Pauli), 31, 78
Landwacht (Home Guard), 55
Lasner, Daniel Otto (Danny), 80
Lasner, Linda Henriette, 80
Lasner, Trude/Trudy. *See* Broessler, Gertrude Maria
League of Nations, xvi
Leidsche Plein, 69
Leopold I, 6
Levin, Herbert, 68
Liberal Party, 33
London, England, 29
London *Times,* 7
Long, Breckenridge, 19–20
Long Island College of Medicine, 79
Lure, France, 48–49

Manhattan, 79
Mariahilf, 17
Mauthausen, 32
Meijer, Johanna Cornelia, 40
Michael Reese Hospital and Medical Center, 79
Michigan City, Indiana, 31, 64, 71–72, 77, 79–80
Milne-Watson, Lord Sir David, 24–25
Milne-Watson, Lady Olga, 24–25
Monongahela River, 79
Montreux, Switzerland, 52
Morton, Gustav, 77
Mrs. Miniver, 70
Munich, Germany, xv
Municipal University of Amsterdam, 33
Mussolini, Benito, xv, 11
Myasthenia Gravis Foundation, 79

Nancy, France, 47–49
National Council of Jewish Women (NCJW), 79
Nazi Germany, 1
Nazi Party, 4, 9, 11
Nazis, 10, 14, 16, 28–34, 36, 45, 50–51, 55–56, 61, 73–74
Nazism, 11
Nederlandsche SS, 55
Netherlands, The (Holland), 20, 23–26, 44–46, 48–49, 51, 55–56, 61, 65–66, 70, 73, 77
New Deal, 31
Newfoundland, 67–68, 71
Newmark, Katya, 81
Newmark, Leonard, 81
Newmark, Mark, 81
Newmark, Ruth. *See* Broessler, Ruth Sylvia
New York, New York, 31, 67, 71, 73, 78–80
Norway, 26
North Africa, 43
Notgeld (paper currency), 4
Nuremberg Laws, 1, 31

Oberman Family, 36
Of Mice and Men, 70
Onderduiker (under diver), 59, 62, 71

Passeur, 44, 50
P.C. Hooftstraat, 69
Pearl Harbor, 64
Pelser, Henk, 47
"Phony War." *See Sitzkrieg*
Pittsburgh, Pennsylvania, 79–80
Pogroms, 32
Poland, 25, 35, 39, 50–51
Pollaczek, Ludwig, 17
Ponlechner, Mitzi (Maria), 8–9, 23
Porrentruy, Switzerland, 50
Portugal, 18, 35
Prague, Czechoslovakia, 62
Putsch, xv, 11
Pyrenees Mountains, 55

Radio City Music Hall, 68
Realgymnasium, 69
Renner, Karl, 3
Rényi, Borka, 19
Révész Family, 65
Révész, Geza, 20
Révész, Magda, 19–20, 22, 38
Ringstrasse Demonstration, 4
Rink, Arnold, 5, 72
Rohrpost (pneumatic mail), 8
Rosendaaal, The Netherlands, 45
Roosevelt Administration, 31
Rotterdam, The Netherlands, 65
Royal Metal, 71
Rue de Jemappes, 46
Rue Jeanne d'Arc, 47

Saccharin, 45
Sann, Mr. and Mrs. Adolphe, 51
Schattendorf, 4
Scheveningen, 30
Schiphol Airport, 70
Sedan, France, 47
Seitz, Karl, 3
Separation Act, 3

Severin Schreibergasse, 5
Seyss-Inquart, Arthur, 28
Simons, Caroline, 23, 62, 77
Simons, Erika Grace Line (Eka), 38–40, 60–61
Simons, Estella (Tante Stel), 35, 39–40, 62, 78
Simons, Euphemia (Phemia), 39
Simons Family, 20, 22, 30–31, 35, 59, 65, 70, 74, 77–78
Simons, Hannie Estella, 23, 62, 77
Simons, Johanna, 39–40, 58–59
Simons, Judith (Tin), 23, 62, 77
Simons, Marianne van Raalte (Oma Simons), 35, 39–40, 78
Simons, Marinus, 23, 62, 77
Simons, Philip, 40
Simons, Siebert, 39, 58
Simons, Sophie Marianne (Jobje), 23, 59–60, 77
Sitzkrieg (phony war), 25
Sixth District (Vienna), 17
Social Democratic Party, 3
Social Democrats, 2–4, 11
Society Lingerie, 31
South Bend, Indiana, 68
Spanish Civil War, xvi
Sperrstempel (exemption stamps), 36
Spitzmann, Rita, 70
Stalingrad, 29
Ständestaat, 11
Stanislas Square, 48
Statue of Liberty, 68, 78
Star of David, 33–34
Stumpergasse, 17
Sturmabteilung (SA), 16
Sugar, Ada, xvi, 5, 72
Sugar, Endre, 5, 71
Sugar, Ernst, xvi, 5
Sugar, Jenny, 5, 71
Süsskind, Walter, 55
Switzerland, 44, 47, 50–52

Taglicht, Edith, 15
Tartakoff, Alan M., 81

Thalheimer, 44
Theresienstadt, 40, 78
The Dictator, xv
Time Capsule, xv
Times Square, 68
Tobruk, 43
Treaty of Saint-Germain-en-Laye, 2

Underground, 23, 55, 58–59
Ungar, Steffi, 16
Union of Soviet Socialist Republics (Soviet Union), 28, 32
United States, 18, 23, 51, 64–69, 71–73, 78
University of Amsterdam, 20
Utrecht, The Netherlands, 35, 37–38, 54, 62, 70, 77

van Blokland, Belaerts, 44
van Saher, Lilla Alexander, 72
Venezuela, 35
Vermögensverkehrstelle (Property Transfer Office), 17
Vienna, Austria, xv, xvi, 1–10, 14, 17, 18, 21, 35, 48, 62, 77–79, 81
Viennese Jews, 6, 10, 17
Visser, Lodewijk, 33
Volkswehr (people's militia), 3
von Saher, Eduard, 72
von Schuschnigg, Kurt, 11, 15
Vrijwilige Hulp-Police (Volunteer Auxillary Police), 55
Vught, 29

Wavre, Belgium, 46
Wehrmacht, 26
Weimar Republic, xvi
Weissenberg, Lisa, 78
Weissenberg, Maria, 78
Weissenberg, Omama (Grandmother), 78
Weissman, Andy, 78, 81
Weissman, Dana (Spurling), 81
Weissman, Eva. *See* Broessler, Eva Gertrud

Weissman, Joshua, 81
Weissman, Judy, 81
Weissman, Oscar, 79–80
Westerbork, 62
Women's Hospital, 72
World War I, xv, xvi, 24
World War II, 24

Yellow Peril, xvi
Young Christian Men's Association (YMCA), 72
Yugoslavia, 2

Zionism, xvi, 55
Zurich, Switzerland, 66

About the Authors

Eva Broessler Weissman escaped from Vienna, Austria, to The Netherlands in 1939. Because a caring family removed her from danger, she survived arrest, and acted as a courier in the Dutch Resistance until the end of the Nazi occupation. After World War II, she was able to move to the United States. She has devoted her life to work in nonprofit organizations and currently lives in Lakewood, Ohio.

Dr. Gregory Moore received his doctorate in History from Kent State University, and is Associate Professor of History and Political Science at Notre Dame College in Cleveland, Ohio. He currently serves as Chair of the Department of History and Political Science and Director of the Center for Intelligence Studies at Notre Dame and lives in Wadsworth, Ohio.

The girl with the dove—a statue in the garden of the Broessler home in Bad Vöslau. The war came to her too, and she also survived, as a reminder of both the family who cherished her and of the peace she symbolizes. Taken by Katya Newmark, April 2008.